LATIN AMERICA

Joanie pp 89-90

SOUTHEAST ASIA by TILLMAN DURDIN

AFRICA by WALDEMAR A. NIELSEN

RUSSIA by HARRISON E. SALISBURY

CHINA by HARRY SCHWARTZ

LATIN AMERICA by TAD SZULC

THE MIDDLE EAST by JAY WALZ

NEW YORK TIMES BYLINE BOOKS

LATIN AMERICA

by Tad Szulc

A NEW YORK TIMES BYLINE BOOK

ATHENEUM

NEW YORK

1966

TO ANTHONY

Copyright © 1965 by The New York Times Company
All rights reserved
Library of Congress catalog card number 65–27528
Published simultaneously in Canada by McClelland and Stewart Ltd.
Manufactured in the United States of America
Composition by H. Wolff, New York
Printed by The Murray Printing Company,
Forge Village, Massachusetts
Designed by Harry Ford
First Printing December 1965
Second Printing March 1966
Third Printing June 1966
Fourth Printing August 1966

CONTENTS

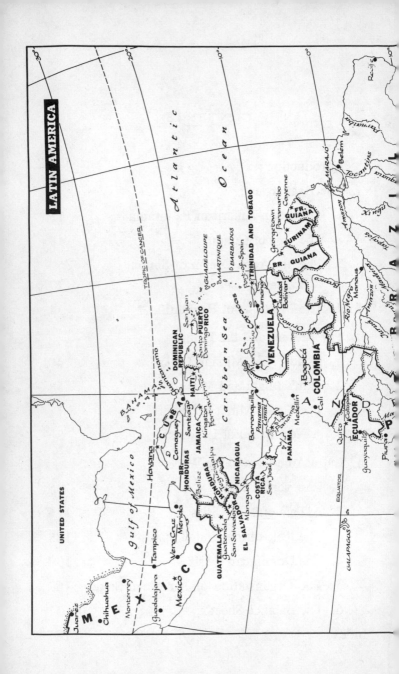

INTRODUCTION

On the afternoon of Saturday, April 24, 1965, I was at work on one of the concluding chapters of this book—one dealing with relations between the United States and Latin America. I had just finished a sentence recalling the occupation of the Dominican Republic by United States Marines in 1916 when my telephone at home in Washington suddenly rang.

It was the Foreign News Editor of *The New York Times* calling from New York. "A revolution seems to have broken out in the Dominican Republic," he said. "Please get on the next plane to Santo Domingo."

I left the following morning, and for the next five weeks I witnessed a bloody and hectic drama, highlighted by the landing of United States Marines in the Dominican Republic almost 49 years after the first such American intervention there.

The intervention of 1965—initially begun, like the one in 1916, to protect foreign lives and restore peace—evoked the same fears and resentments of the United States in Latin America that had existed nearly a half-century ago.

But to make matters worse this time, in sharp contrast to 1916, the concept of military intervention was no longer acceptable in the Western Hemisphere. The United States had long ago renounced its self-appointed right to intervene in Latin American affairs. That policy of intervention, dating back to Teddy Roosevelt and the imperialistic Manifest Destiny slogan of the 19th century, was presumably gone forever. Moreover the Charter of the Organization of American States now specifically banned such unilateral acts.

On the other hand, the United States was now living in a vastly more complicated and dangerous world. Cuba, the Caribbean neighbor of the island of Hispaniola, which the Dominican Republic shares with Haiti, had fallen under Communist domination only a few years earlier. Communist subversion was a new fact of international relations, changing everywhere the old definitions of aggression and therefore the patterns of response to it.

Thus, the landing of American Marines and paratroopers in the Dominican Republic late in April, 1965, became one of the most controversial actions of the United States in recent decades. The move has been denounced as a rash and thoughtless one, based on insufficient evidence of a Communist conspiracy to take over the Dominican revolt. It has been defended in Washington as inevitable to preclude the creation of "another Cuba."

The historians will have the final word in judging the course President Johnson took. Nevertheless the Dominican affair constitutes a great milestone in U.S. relations with Latin America, for the intervention of 1965 dramatically refashioned inter-American concepts. It brought about the creation of an inter-American armed force—a regional equivalent of the United Nations peacekeeping forces elsewhere in the world. In all likelihood it also put an end to the cherished notion that the principle of nonintervention is inviolable in any and all circumstances. In addition it underlined the depth of United States involvement and responsibilities in Latin America.

Troubled by the problems of Europe and Asia, the United States seemed unaware of the rising pressures in its own backyard until a dramatic event in inter-American relations occurred on May 13, 1958. On that date Richard M. Nixon, then Vice

President of the United States, was spat upon and nearly lynched by a maddened crowd in Caracas, Venezuela.

As a correspondent for *The Times* covering the Nixon trip I was in the vehicle immediately ahead of the Vice Presidential limousine during the mob charge on the motorcade. This was my first major exposure to the intensity of Latin-American feelings about the United States and I shall long remember it as a symbol of the extraordinary difficulties faced by this country in seeking to live with what has come to be called the Latin-American revolution.

Caracas was the final stop on the Nixon tour, which had been undertaken to demonstrate the goodwill of the United States toward Latin America. Instead it produced an explosion of all the Latin-American frustrations against the U.S. The Nixon party had been spat upon and insulted in Lima, Peru, a few days earlier, and in other cities it had also felt the hostility of the crowds. Nonetheless, the explosion that engulfed the Vice President in Caracas came as a grim surprise to me even though I had traveled throughout Latin America for *The Times* since 1956 and knew well the rising wave of discontent in that huge portion of the globe.

Dramatic as the Nixon incident was, events that followed seemed to dwarf it. Seven months later —on January 1, 1959—a bearded guerrilla fighter named Fidel Castro took power in Cuba, and all at once the whole pattern of Latin America appeared to change. Revolution became the overriding slogan everywhere. And the seeds of the Dominican strife that was to erupt more than six years later were sown in part by the Cuban revolution and its consequences.

Late in 1959 I once sat up all night with Castro, first in a hotel kitchen, then on a deserted beach and finally in a cafeteria as the sun rose over Havana, listening to him predict a wave of Latin-American revolutions. "They must come," he said, gesturing with both arms, "and the influence of the United States will vanish forever."

It soon became clear, however, that while a revolutionary wave was indeed sweeping over Latin America, it was not necessarily of the sort Castro had in mind. Latin America wanted change, yes, but not Communism as a patent medicine for her terribly deep ills.

The crying need was for economic development and social justice, for land reform to change the ownership patterns that had prevailed for centuries, for more jobs, housing, schools and hospitals for fast-growing populations. There was also a desire for political liberty under democratic systems. And if anything was certain, it was that the 220 million Latin Americans would no longer wait passively for a better life. They were ready to do something about poverty, misery, hunger, illiteracy, disease and dictatorships—the old curses of the masses.

In March, 1961, a young American President sought to offer a way out. John F. Kennedy invited Latin America to join the United States in a "vast effort, unparalleled in magnitude and nobility of purpose, to satisfy the basic needs" of the Latin-American people "for homes, work and land, health and schools." Thus he launched the Alliance for Progress, a program of economic development within the framework of democracy that has already begun to change the face of Latin America.

I have revisited Latin America a number of times since the Alliance was set in motion, most recently when the Dominican explosion seemed to raise again the question of whether peaceful democratic revolutions—as visualized by President Kennedy—were indeed possible.

Even before the Dominican crisis many Latin Americans were skeptical about the Alliance. Among intellectuals and students there was grumbling that it was a new vehicle for "Yankee imperialism." Statesmen complained that it was not moving fast enough. Wealthy landowners feared it was a "socialistic" scheme that would ruin them.

But despite the impatient and superficial judgments, the Alliance is the symbol of a very real new approach to Latin-American problems. A new breed of Latin Americans—the young economists, engineers and "technocrats"—are making the first comprehensive effort to remedy the old ills of their nations.

With the Alliance pioneering basic new techniques, economic development is being planned rationally with a sense of the real needs of the people. Land reform is a fact in several countries, and laws leading to it have been approved in a dozen others. Education—both in quality and the number of new institutions—is on the upswing. New industry is emerging, from Peru in the west to Brazil in the east.

Yet Latin America still suffers from dangerous instability, as the events of recent years keep reminding us. Caracas is still living with the terrorism of pro-Castro snipers. In Brazil the government was overthrown by the military in April, 1964, to save the country from chaos. In Bolivia a regime that was once dedicated to social reform bogged down in personal quarrels and corruption and was ousted by the army in November, 1964. Six months later open warfare flared between the military and the miners and workers. In Colombia leftist conspiracies and street battles between students and the police led to the imposition of a state of siege in May, 1965. And, most dramatic of all, the Dominican Republic broke down under a bloody civil war in April and May, 1965, leading to the landing of American troops.

Thus, the spectacular rebellions and the quiet basic efforts at economic and social development are the parallel themes of today's Latin America. Together they add up to the continuing fundamental revolution of this vast area as it strives to hurry into the modern age.

I The Background

I

The Latin-American
Panorama

"LATIN AMERICA" is a label of convenience for a collection of immensely varied lands. The part of the world we call "Latin America" was colonized by no fewer than five European powers. It speaks today four main languages and a half-dozen dialects. It is cursed and blessed by climates ranging from exhausting tropical heat to fine temperate weather. It is endowed with fertile regions and plagued by impassable jungles and mountain chains. Part of it is in the jet and electronics age and part of it is in the prediscovery era of 500 years ago. It is by no means a cohesive entity.

Yet this amazing and contradictory Latin America does share a common aim: to overcome chronic economic and social underdevelopment and, in so doing, to present a reasonably united front toward North America, Europe, Africa and Asia. Despite tremendous differences from country to country, the modernizing forces at work press increasingly in the direction of greater unity, not away from it.

Latin America is divided into four main groupings: the continent of South America, the isthmus of Central America, the Republic of Mexico (which is geographically part of North America) and the islands of the Caribbean. Linguistically Latin America is split into 18 Spanish-speaking lands, Portuguese-speaking Brazil, Creole-speaking Haiti and the English-speaking countries and colonies of the Caribbean. Five or six widely spoken Indian dialects still survive in South America and to some extent in Central America, and a great many people are bilingual in Spanish or Portuguese and an Indian tongue. Haiti's commonly spoken and highly picturesque Creole is based on French but incorporates words from several languages, including African ones. There is Dutch-influenced speech in the Netherlands Antilles, while in the linguistic babel of British Guiana and Trinidad the dialects of East Indians and even Chinese (who were imported as laborers) coexist with a lilting English plus Spanish and Portuguese.

For a reporter a good command of Spanish is not enough: certain words and expressions mean one thing in the Caribbean area and precisely the opposite in the southern part of South America. Incidentally, the Brazilians understand Spanish, but the Spanish-speaking peoples barely comprehend Portuguese. As for Creole, even native Frenchmen find themselves completely lost.

Politically Latin America is composed of 22 sovereign republics and a handful of more or less disputed British, French and Dutch possessions.

In South America the republics are Argentina, Bolivia, Brazil, Chile, Colombia, Ecuador, Panama (often considered part of Central America), Paraguay, Peru, Uruguay and Venezuela. In Central America they are Costa Rica, El Salvador, Guatemala, Honduras and Nicaragua. Then to the north comes Mexico. In the Caribbean the republics are Cuba, the Dominican Republic, Haiti and the newly independent Jamaica, Trinidad and Tobago.

Tucked away in Central America is the colony of British Honduras, which Guatemala claims and calls Belize. On the northeastern shoulder of South America are the colonies of British Guiana and French Guiana (the latter once famous for its Devil's Island penal institution). Between the Guianas is Surinam, formerly known as Dutch Guiana, now a self-governing territory. In the bleakness of the far South Atlantic are the British Falkland Islands, which the Argentines call the Malvinas and demand for themselves.

In the Caribbean the French possessions are Martinique and Guadeloupe and a handful of smaller islands. The British hold the Bahamas, Barbados and about 3,000 other islands, islets and sandspits. The Netherlands controls the islands of the Dutch West Indies. And, finally, the United States flag flies over the Commonwealth of Puerto Rico, the Territory of the Virgin Islands and the tiny Great Corn and Little Corn Islands, these last two leased from Nicaragua. This multinational flavor of the Caribbean reflects the European wars of the 16th to 18th centuries, the corsair raids of those days and the Spanish-American War, fought in 1898.

Diverse and seemingly unrelated, all these countries, colonies and territories, with their blends of white, Indian, Negro, East Indian and other peoples, fit nonetheless into the broad concept of what we call Latin America. If there is a single common denominator, it is, I believe, their sense of being part of the idea of Latin America, of the striving to break the shackles of underdevelopment, of the struggle to teach, to feed, to house, to decently employ and otherwise care for rapidly expanding populations. This area-wide effort accounts for the revolutionary pressures sweeping Latin America from Communist Cuba to the heartland of South America, for the restlessness and instability of virtually every republic and for their experiments with diverse political forms ranging from representative democracy at its best to archaic military dictatorship at its worst.

Latin America is today, then, still in search of her destiny. It is a search that began nearly 500 adventurous years ago when Admiral Christopher Columbus first sailed into the Caribbean on behalf of the Queen of Spain in quest of the gold and spices of India.

II

The Age of Conquest

COLUMBUS DISCOVERED the New World when he came upon one of the Bahamas on October 12, 1492, and then proceeded to Hispaniola, the island that today is divided between the Dominican Republic and Haiti. But long before Columbus there already existed magnificent civilizations in what we now call Latin America.

The great Indian cultures—the Aztec in Mexico, the Mayan in Central America and the Inca in western South America—were born in mysterious ways when Europe was still in her barbarian stage, a millennium or more before the birth of Christ. It is assumed that the New World Indian cultures were flourishing 2,000 years ago, though no archeological research has thus far been able to pinpoint their origin. Historians generally accept the theory that the Indians of Latin America are the descendants of Mongol peoples who crossed the Bering Straits from Asia into North America about 20,000 years ago, after the Wisconsin glacial epoch. Some of them remained in North America while others continued moving south, migrating into Mexico and Central America, onto the Caribbean islands and to the South American continent, all the way to Tierra del Fuego, the world's southernmost inhabited area.

This does not explain, of course, how some of these Indian nations were able to construct intricate civilizations, rivaling in many ways those of ancient Egypt, while others remained backward for centuries—in fact, until now. To this day Latin America's jungles are the home of naked savages who have not yet even fully entered the Stone Age. Why the Indians of Latin America developed in such an uneven manner remains a deep mystery. But after the Spanish conquest, tragically, all the great Indian civilizations vanished and primitiveness became universal.

The first contact between the peoples of the Old World and the New took place on the shores of Hispaniola, where Columbus came upon savage Indians who later massacred the small garrison he left behind between his first and second voyages. But when Cortez landed in Yucatán in 1519 to begin the conquest of Mexico and Pizarro came ashore on the

Ecuadorean coast in 1531 to start the conquest of Peru, the medieval Spaniards collided with cultures in many ways superior to their own.

In this collision Christian influence played its role along with the conquerors' weapons. Priests and monks accompanied the Spaniards; they likewise went with the Portuguese into what today is Brazil. The men of the cloth were often the chroniclers of the expeditions, but their foremost task was the conversion of the natives to Christianity. In so doing they secured Latin America for Roman Catholicism.

The conquest of Mexico and Peru is a great but also terrible tale. In opening up the New World, the Spanish soldiers wrought military and diplomatic miracles and performed extraordinary feats of human endurance. Yet they brought about the collapse not only of the Indian empires but also of whole cultures. Today, more than 400 years after Cortez vanquished Montezuma, the Aztec emperor, in order to conquer Mexico—and more than 400 years after Pizarro put the last Inca emperor to death in order to secure Spain's rule over the Andes—the Indian populations have still not regained the degree of civilization and well-being they enjoyed at the time of the conquest.

I remember talking one day to a South American expert in Indian affairs in a tiny village high in the Ecuadorean sierra. I was working on a magazine ar-

ticle for *The Times,* and we inspected the Indians'
filthy windowless shacks, similar to those of hundreds of other Andean villages. I listened uncom-
prehendingly to my friend's conversation with the
village elders in their quick, guttural Quechua dialect. Sighing deeply, he then turned to me: "If we
could only bring them back to the Inca days . . .
then we wouldn't have any problems in fitting them
into the 20th century."

The advanced state of civilization the Incas had
attained is still evident today. High in the Andes
above Cuzco, Peru, which had been the capital of
Atahualpa's empire, there rises the fantastic city of
Machu Picchu, a stone fortress that is like a mirage
among the mountain peaks. Built perhaps around
1000 A.D. or earlier, it is one of the engineering and
architectural marvels of the world, more impressive
in its own fierce way than the pyramids.

The Inca road network across the Andes, unify-
ing the various sections of an empire that once
spread from what is now southern Colombia to
northern Argentina, is a striking reminder that six
or seven centuries ago men using only crude tools
carved out roads that today's engineers could not
duplicate even with bulldozers and dynamite. Peru's
young president, Fernando Belaúnde Terry, whose
great dream is an international highway running
along the Andes, once told me that he hopes only
to be able to do what his Indian forefathers did.

The remains of irrigation works and the fantastic geometric tracing having to do with the movements of the sun and the moon in relation to time and the calendar are but some monuments to Inca science and ingenuity at a time when Europe was still in the Dark Ages. The ruins of Mayan and Aztec towns testify to skill in architecture and mathematics, to advanced social and political organizations and to talents in working gold, silver, copper and other metals in what is now a forgotten era.

But if the Indian civilizations immediately preceding the conquest must inspire admiration (and one should remember that even the Incas came after the fairly advanced Chimu and Chibcha cultures at the dawn of recorded history), the feats of the Spanish conquistadors likewise deserve note.

It takes an airplane flight over the Andes to comprehend fully the magnitude of the Spaniards' endurance. The heavily armored soldiers and their horses had to ascend mountains up to 20,000 feet to reach the strongholds of the Inca empire. Then, a mere handful of men, they swiftly destroyed it. The conquistadors succeeded far from the Andes, too. Balboa had crossed the steaming jungles of Panama to stand on the shores of the Pacific. Other Spaniards made their way along the Amazon and the Orinoco and out into the empty plains radiating from the River Plate.

For all practical purposes, the conquest of Latin

America was completed during the 16th century. While the Spaniards busied themselves settling the islands of the Caribbean and moving down the west coast of South America, Pedro Alvarez Cabral and other Portuguese navigators were staking out their claims on the continent's east coast in the vast area of what is now Brazil. Because successive papal rulings and the Treaty of Tordesillas effectively divided the New World between the crowns of Spain and Portugal, the colonizing efforts of these two countries developed side by side without visible friction, creating different forms of society. The cultural seeds planted by the Spaniards in their colonies and by the Portuguese in Brazil have thus produced nations that today are remarkably dissimilar except for their common economic interests.

Latin America did not escape other European influences. The French and the Dutch repeatedly raided the Brazilian coast, establishing and briefly holding settlements. These incursions had considerable cultural impact, and today French and Dutch names are part of the Brazilian heritage. Moreover, France and the Netherlands obtained colonies in northeastern South America that are now French Guiana and Surinam. In the Caribbean the raids of the British privateers and the English-Spanish wars put the Union Jack in the West Indies, so named because it was India that Columbus had sought in the first place.

For 300 years Latin America developed as a source of raw materials for the Old World. The colonies provided gold and silver, precious stones, timber (Brazil acquired its name from the Pau Brasil wood) and later sugar, coffee, cotton and the industrial metals required by Europe. The land was given in grants by the Spanish and Portuguese crowns to the viceroys and captains, the deserving noblemen and enterprising merchants. The heartland of South America began to open up with the expeditions of the Brazilian trailblazers and their counterparts from Peru, Chile and Argentina.

New societies started to emerge. The Spanish and Portuguese conquerors were followed by settlers who began to marry among themselves and often with the Indians. At the outset of the 17th century, slave ships from Africa began bringing tremendous numbers of Negroes to Brazil, the Caribbean and northern South America for forced labor. In the years since then the African cultural influence has become intermixed with the Indian and white, dominating some societies, as in Haiti and parts of Brazil, Cuba and the West Indies, and playing an important role elsewhere in the Latin-American melting pot. The African origins of Cuban and other Caribbean music and of the Brazilian samba and batuque are obvious manifestations of this heritage. Today it is no accident that countries like Brazil, Cuba and Haiti, though each for its own political reasons, are reaching out for special relationships with Africa.

The immense wealth of the colonial aristocracy —the officials and the planters—came into being alongside the misery of the native Indian populations, the imported Negro slaves and the less privileged settlers and manual laborers. The colonizers sought to extract as much wealth as possible for their overseas masters rather than to develop the economies of the colonies, which meant that emphasis was placed entirely on exportable crops and products. The result of this policy is the awesome economic distortion from which Latin America suffers today and the deep chasm between the haves and have-nots. The current revolutionary situations in the Western Hemisphere can be traced back to the Spanish, Portuguese and French colonial practices.

Meanwhile great cities, patterned on those in the Old World but incorporating New World influences, began rising throughout Latin America: the viceregal capital of Lima, the very Europeanized Buenos Aires, the Portuguese-inspired Rio de Janeiro and the Aztec-Spanish Mexico City. It was the period of magnificent colonial architecture, with colonial art developing its own individuality. Great churches were erected and with them came superb works of religious art, like the dark paintings of the Quito School. The colonial monuments, which form a bridge between the Indian past and the exploding modernity of the present, are still to be seen throughout Latin America, providing still another facet of this many-faceted area.

As the 18th century drew to a close, Latin America's colonization was complete and her riches had made her a great prize. But before other European powers could seek to wrest this prize away from the colonizers, the colonies themselves began to stir with a desire for independence. The American Revolution of 1776 and the French Revolution of 1789 were the great events that helped awaken the hunger for liberty. Latin America now stood on the threshold of the Age of Emancipation. She was soon to attain political freedom. What is tragic is that she lost a great chance to achieve political union. This failure of many new nations to combine into a single entity on the order of the United States was to cost her dearly—to this very day.

III

The Shattered Dream of Simón Bolívar

`HE FIRST QUARTER of the 19th century, with its rebellions and protracted wars of independence, fired Latin America with a new sense of destiny, pride and patriotism that still lives on in heroic monuments, historical legends and impassioned oratory.

The uprisings against Spanish, Portuguese and French rule also assured Latin America of her own pantheon of heroes. There was Simón Bolívar, the liberator of Venezuela, Colombia and Peru, a figure of courage, wisdom, romance and tragedy. Statues of him in bronze and stone, usually astride a galloping steed, dot cities from Lima to Caracas, his birthplace. The Republic of Bolivia is named after him. So is the currency of Venezuela, the bolivar. Then there was Argentina's José de San Martín, who crossed the Andes into Chile to carry the torch of independence to the Pacific Coast. Bernardo O'Higgins, the Irishman, helped liberate Chile and then joined forces with San Martín to carry the freedom war north to Peru.

And there were others, among them Jean Jacques Dessalines, the Negro slave who dramatically tore the white rectangle out of the French tricolor to create Haiti's blue-and-red flag and signify the end of colonial rule in 1804, making Haiti the first independent country of Latin America. In Brazil there was the ascetic Tiradentes, leader of the Inconfidência Mineira movement against Portugal, whose body was hacked to pieces after he was hanged for plotting against the crown. And there was José Martí of Cuba, the poet-patriot who helped lead his island to independence from Spain at the turn of the 20th century, thus completing the cycle of the emancipation movements.

Latin America's liberation was a long, bloody and seesawing battle. The Spanish armies often threatened to smash the bands of patriots and sometimes succeeded, for the Spaniards fought as hard to keep Latin America as they had fought three centuries earlier to conquer it. But the thrust for independence came from the direct descendants of the early conquerors, the aristocratic Criollo leaders born in the New World of Spanish forebears. It was a desperate combat between two branches of the same conquering family, and in the end the Criollos won.

Only Brazil escaped the bloodshed of the liberation wars. Although the Tiradentes rebellion was brutally smashed, Portugal agreed less than 50 years later to a peaceful transition of sovereignty. The son of Portugal's King João XXVI became emperor of an independent Brazil in 1822 under the name of Pedro I, and in 1889 a bloodless revolution established the republic.

The grievances that brought about Latin America's struggle for independence were similar to those which led the North American colonists to rise against King George III of England. Thus as early as 1765 the population of Quito in the vice-royalty of New Granada rebelled against the establishment of liquor monopoly and drove the Spaniards out of the city. In 1776 riots against new taxes erupted in New Granada and then in the vice-royalty of Peru and the captaincy-general of Chile. Four years later a widespread Indian revolt broke out in Peru against the Spaniards and their allies of the moment, the Criollo landowners, over the system of forced labor for the Indians.

This rebellion was put down, but by then the Criollo leaders were ready to assume command of the anti-Spanish struggle. In 1781 they rose in New Granada and proclaimed it an independent republic. Spain succeeded in crushing this uprising, but it became a turning point in Latin-American history. It marked the real beginning of the movements to separate Latin America from her mother countries.

By 1822 virtually all of Latin America had shed colonial rule and the newly independent lands stood at the doorway to destiny. This destiny might have been political union, or at least a union of the Spanish-speaking countries, and had it been achieved the subsequent history of Latin America would be strikingly different. But union was only a dream of Simón Bolívar, the man who understood Latin America's future better than anyone else in his time, and the dream quickly succumbed to the realities of jealousies and intrigues. Yet there did exist a chance for a unified southern continent, short-lived as it was.

After liberating Venezuela, New Granada and Ecuador, Bolívar succeeded in forming a federated nation extending from the Pacific Coast over the forbidding ridges of the Andes to the Caribbean. The Congresses of Angostura and Cucuta in 1819 and 1821 formally proclaimed this the Republic of Great Colombia with Bolívar its first president. Panama joined and Bolívar turned south in an attempt to extend his federation.

In July, 1822, he traveled to the sleepy, hot Ecuadorean port of Guayaquil to meet with San Martín, who had marched north from Lima, and their conference loomed as a prelude to a continental union. But instead the two great liberators clashed over plans for a joint campaign against what remained of Spain's position in South America. In the end San Martín withdrew to Chile and then to his native Argentina, leaving to an embittered Bolívar the task of completing the liberation of Peru.

Bolívar found temporary solace in Central America. There the captaincies-general of the isthmus proclaimed in 1823 the short-lived Federal Republic of Central America and talk arose that it might unite with Bolívar's Great Colombia. On the island of Hispaniola, Santo Domingo, now the Dominican Republic, made a move to join Great Colombia, but the Haitians prevented this by invading Santo Domingo.

At the end of 1823 the United States, which had recognized the independence of Latin America, proclaimed the Monroe Doctrine. This warned against any efforts by European nations to regain their positions in the New World. It also represented a potential influence toward political unification.

Bolívar sought to take advantage of it—and to try to strengthen his concept of federation—by convening the Congress of Panama in 1826. But only a few governments sent delegates and this attempt, too, foundered. When Bolívar, a disillusioned and broken man, died a few years later, he had not only failed to unify Latin America but had also seen his Great Colombian federation coming apart under the powerful pressures of new nationalisms.

Having been unable to attain unity, Latin America embarked on a century of warfare, revolutions and instability so great as to prevent any meaningful progress. Already beset by awesome problems of climate and geography, Latin America succeeded in paralyzing herself politically and this political paralysis led to economic and social stagnation.

Colombia warred against Peru. Peru, in turn, fought Chile. Paraguay was set upon by Argentina, Brazil and Uruguay. Later, Brazilians and Argentines fought each other. As late as the nineteen-thirties Bolivia and Paraguay engaged in a long bloody war in which each was backed by international petroleum interests. In the early nineteen-forties Peru and Ecuador fought a war over Ecuador's northeastern provinces. To this day their border problem has not been solved and it goes on poisoning their relations.

The Latin-American republics, despite constitutions patterned on that of the United States, were ruled by tiny elites, with dictators and warlords succeeding each other in a bloody game of musical chairs. It was not until 1948 that a constitutional president of Ecuador was allowed to complete a full term in office—but the continuity of lawful rule was broken again in 1962. Venezuela, which lived from 1908 to 1935 under the dictatorship of Juan Vicente Gómez, the "Tyrant of the Andes," did not see a president complete his term until 1964.

Economically Latin America was—and still is to a large extent—a collection of small islands of prosperity in an ocean of misery. Only a few years ago, as the rumbles of the great social revolutions of the nineteen-sixties began to be heard in the region, were the first steps taken to help Latin America along the road of rational development. One hundred and forty years after Simón Bolívar's failure to unite Latin America politically, a climate favorable to economic integration is finally developing, and it may be hoped that this will prove the first step toward some form of political union.

But much of Latin America still has a foot in the woeful past—and the revolutionary rumblings grow louder each day.

IV

The Mystique of Revolution

EVEN BEFORE Fidel Castro took power in Cuba in January, 1959, "Revolution"—always with a capital "R"—was already a household word in Latin America. Since then it has unquestionably become the most commonly used political term—though it means different things to different people.

Touring Latin America late in 1961 on a *New York Times* assignment, I became so conscious of the use and abuse of the word "Revolution" in political speeches and newspaper editorials that I amused myself for several weeks in a number of capitals by keeping count of every mention of it. My informal survey disclosed that "Revolution" had been uttered as many as a dozen times by every speaker I had heard, no matter what the context.

There were calls for the "Revolution," descriptions of the "Revolution" and statements that "the Revolution is already here."

I remember mentioning this to a shrewd and cynical Latin-American editor of my acquaintance. His reaction was that "today you have to be for Revolution, whatever that means, just as you are for God, country and family, if you want to succeed in Latin-American politics."

Covering in 1962 the first free elections which the Dominican Republic had held in thirty-eight years, I counted six political parties with "Revolution" or "Revolutionary" in their names. There was the Dominican Revolutionary party, the Revolutionary Vanguard and so on. The election of Jânio Quadros as president of Brazil by a landslide in 1960 became known as the "White Revolution," the revolution by ballot instead of bullet. The overthrow by the army in 1964 of João Goulart, the successor of Quadros (who had resigned after seven months in office), was heralded as the "true Brazilian Revolution." President Eduardo Frei Montalva of Chile defeated a Marxist opponent in the 1964 election by campaigning on a platform of "Revolution with Liberty."

To be sure, "Revolution" is not a new word or a new concept in Latin America. The difference today is that it is used in a new sense relating to the need for profound social changes. In the 18th and 19th

centuries "Revolution" was applied to the struggles
for independence. Later it was invoked every time a
change in government was being justified by the
"outs" against the "ins."

Then as now the word electrified the masses, often sending them into the streets to battle against
one usurper for a new usurper. In fact, the mystique
of "Revolution" is one of the underlying traditions
of restless Latin America. To be a revolutionary,
successful or not, even to go to prison for conspiracy , is a badge of honor for students and teachers,
sergeants and generals, intellectuals and professional politicians.

The Latin American scene is crowded with political figures, often presidents and cabinet ministers,
who are proud of the time they spent in jail for con-
spiring against those whom they considered tyrants,
usurpers or dictators. Peru's constitutional president, Fernando Belaúnde Terry, was briefly a prisoner some years ago. Venezuela's president, Raúl
Leoni, and his predecessor, Rómulo Betancourt,
both served long prison terms as student agitators
against the Gómez tyranny. In Brazil the Communist party leader Luiz Carlos Prestes was elected to
the Senate in 1946 after he had spent nine years in
prison. In 1964 he was again in hiding. As a correspondent in Latin America one becomes accustomed to interviewing newsworthy men in jail. I remember having coffee in a Chilean prison in 1956

with the incarcerated labor leader Clotario Blest, who apologized for receiving me in such an inelegant place. In Colombia I played chess with a prominent political prisoner.

Often Latin-American politicians seek protection at foreign embassies when a government falls or a rebellion fails. To facilitate this, Latin-American jurisprudence long ago came up with the concept of asylum—so sacred a principle that even so tough a foe of Latin-American traditions as Cuba's Castro has respected it over the years. An inter-American convention covers the right of asylum and it is almost unheard of for a government to invade a foreign embassy to seize a person who has taken refuge there.

Often, however, a government will refuse to grant an asylee a safe-conduct out of the country. This has led to some extraordinary situations. The most celebrated case is that of Víctor Raúl Haya de la Torre, the founder of the APRA party in Peru, who spent more than five years in the Colombian Embassy in Lima because the Peruvian military regime refused in 1948 to issue him a safe-conduct. For years the embassy building was surrounded by Peruvian troops, some of them in trenches, to prevent Haya de la Torre from escaping. His freedom was eventually negotiated.

In 1955 Argentina's deposed dictator Juan D. Perón hid briefly aboard a Paraguayan gunboat in the Buenos Aires harbor until he was allowed to move on to the Paraguayan Embassy and thence to Paraguay and exile. During the 1958 revolution against the dictatorship of Marcos Pérez Jiménez in Venezuela, correspondents kept scorecards on which politicians would go to which embassy and when. The same happened in Cuba under the Fulgencio Batista dictatorship and again under Castro. Once Castro was in power the grapevine established which Latin-American embassies were "good" or comfortable and the regime's foes often calmly discussed whether it would be "Argentina or Brazil or Venezuela." On one memorable occasion a whole bus jampacked with prospective asylees drove into the garden of the Uruguayan Embassy, right through the rosebush hedges. Soon most Latin-American embassies became so filled with refugees, hundreds in some cases, that the diplomatic staffs had to move elsewhere and the feeding and care of the asylees became a serious problem. But as one Latin-American government after another severed relations with Castro and the embassies were closed, the asylees were finally allowed to go abroad.

The fact that the principle of asylum is so firmly established in Latin America illustrates the inherent instability of the region. But where past revolutions —even the cycle of antidictatorial rebellions in the nineteen-fifties—were largely political, revolution today is increasingly concerned with the mounting economic and social problems besetting the great mass of the people.

Social revolution, of course, is not a complete novelty in Latin America. Mexico had her trailblazing upheaval in 1910. Getúlio Vargas's revolution in Brazil in 1930 led to profound social changes there. Perón's dictatorship in Argentina between 1946 and 1955 was an attempt at social revolution and was based on the support of organized labor. Despite Perón's ouster, millions of Argentines are still voting for *peronismo,* presumably signifying that a social revolution remains desirable. Bolivia lived through a bloody social revolution in 1952, implementing a land reform. And, finally, the Cuban revolution of 1959 was primarily a social-economic upheaval, marking the start of a new era.

The key to the current revolutionary surge throughout Latin America is the feeling, widespread perhaps for the first time, that man can and should do something about the misery of the masses—with a gun or a planner's slide rule.

If one searches for the central problem, it inevitably turns out to be population pressure. Latin America is now the fastest-growing region in the world. Its annual birth rate of more than 3 per cent considerably exceeds that of China, India or Africa. A United States population expert was astounded recently to discover that the birth rate in Costa Rica had reached 4.9 per cent in 1963, a world record. By contrast the United States birth rate is only 1.6 per cent.

Latin America's population explosion, if unchecked, means an increase from about 225 million people in 1965 to more than 600 million by the year 2000. Considering that Latin America is unable even now to feed, house and employ her present population decently, it does not take much imagination to envision the havoc in a generation or two if far-reaching economic and social reforms are not undertaken at once. The population rise, not matched by an increase in production, has already resulted in less food per inhabitant. With much of the population eating inadequately, the specter of starvation is not too far away. Throughout Latin America one encounters throngs of ill-fed, sickly and virtually abandoned children. Often they are naked or in rags when they become too old to go about nude. They scavenge in refuse, play in open sewers and grow up to perpetuate in greater numbers the cycle of misery. It is what Oscar Lewis, the anthropologist, calls the "Culture of Poverty," the handing of poverty and all the evils that go with it from generation to generation. One finds these children in the terrible slums of the great cities, begging in the streets or learning how to steal. In the rural areas one sees them wallowing in dirt in front of their parents' miserable shacks, their bellies distended from gastric diseases and their big eyes blankly expressive. And everywhere one goes there are children and children and more children.

It should be recorded that at least 11 million of these children are able to go to school, where school is available, and are given a better chance to survive childhood because of the food made available to them by the United States under its Food-for-Peace program. To donate food to hungry children does not correct the basic economic distortions of Latin America, but it helps sustain the newest generation as the efforts of the Alliance for Progress to reshape the future get under way.

The current revolutionary trends constitute a protest against the conditions of neglect that prevail in Latin America despite roughly 150 years of independence. It is not surprising that man resolves to listen to revolutionary blandishments from any side after watching his children grow up in squalor without apparent hope of a better tomorrow. I have talked to Peruvians who came down to the coast from the drought-plagued highlands to find work and a new life. What they found, for the most part, is the horrible slums around Lima, and one father told me: "I would rather grab a gun and impose my kind of justice than see my children starve." One hears the same thing in the northeastern region of Brazil, in the slums of Rio de Janeiro, in the villages of Haiti and the mountains of Bolivia. If there is a single great fact about Latin America today, it is that her people are no longer prepared to accept the status quo of misery.

But why is this vast region, so rich in resources, faring so badly in a developing world? Why was so little accomplished in the century and a half of independence? The answers are many, and one may well begin with terrain and weather: the thick jungles covering much of the area, the forbidding Andes and the debilitating tropical climate over a great deal of South America.

As important as the ravages of nature were the ravages of man. The Spaniards destroyed the Aztec, Mayan and Inca empires, but put nothing comparable in terms of civilization in their place. Instead the Spanish and the Portuguese crowns exploited everything they could in the colonies and neglected all the rest.

After independence irresponsible rule continued. In each new republic emphasis was placed on export crops and commodities: sugar, coffee, cocoa, bananas, rubber (for a while) and certain metals. These exports produced wealth for the elite, but no serious attempt was made in 150 years to develop anything that would benefit the whole of society, such as the cultivation of farm staples. The agricultural system was based on absentee landlords, who frequently held tenants in virtual bondage. Those who did not toil on the landlords' haciendas eked out a bare living from tiny plots of almost unproductive land wrested from jungle or mountainside.

I think that what I shall always remember most about remote Latin-American villages is the pungent smell of smoke. Outside there is the smoke from the smoldering fires the peasants light to burn away the forest growth, clearing an acre or two of poor land to plant enough yucca or beans to feed themselves and their families. And inside the windowless huts there is the smoke from the cooking fires—a smoke that pervades things, people and animals. The smell of smoke is the smell of misery. Somehow it also conveys the utter isolation of so much of Latin America—the physical, geographic and economic isolation of populations that never earn or spend money. Because they produce only for their own subsistence, they are neither producers nor consumers in the accepted sense of those words: they have nothing to sell, therefore they can buy nothing. The best they can do is engage in a little barter when, on occasion, their isolation is broken briefly by the appearance of the itinerant merchant in a village with his mule or burro to trade salt, sugar, matches, trinkets or implements for whatever local produce may be in surplus. Afterward the village again lapses into its isolation.

This being to an overwhelming extent the basis of the rural economy, it is small wonder that in 1964, with millions more mouths to feed, Latin America produced less food per inhabitant than in 1948.

This is another way of saying that in 16 years the area regressed in this vital field of endeavor instead of advancing.

The land problem and the problem of food production are the keys to Latin America's future. But to solve those problems and end the cycle of misery it is necessary to reorient the ruling groups and educate the masses. More to eat, more jobs, better housing and better health are needed to create the conditions in which men, women and children can begin to lead decent lives. An attempt at such a breakthrough began in 1961 with the Alliance for Progress, a program of self-help and rational economic planning supported by United States financial aid.

Yet even this new effort constantly runs into awesome obstacles: inflation, excessively heavy foreign debt obligations and the slumping prices of Latin-American commodities.

Inflation is widespread and in Brazil it more than doubled the cost of living in 1963 and 1964. Latin America's foreign debt in 1965 was a staggering $10 billion. And the region's export revenues are dropping while the prices of industrial equipment, which must be purchased abroad to push ahead with economic development, are rising.

In these circumstances it is indeed remarkable that in 1964 Latin America as a whole increased annual per-capita incomes by more than 3 per cent, slightly better than the goal of the Alliance for Progress.

The economic and social pressures and the whole thrust of the breakthrough effort are inevitably resulting in still another phase of political instability. Following the collapse of most of the army-backed dictatorships in the nineteen-fifties, military-dominated governments are returning in the nineteen-sixties. Between 1961 and 1964 six such regimes emerged in Latin America, taking power in Guatemala, Honduras, the Dominican Republic, Brazil, Bolivia and Ecuador.

Unlike the regimes of 10 or 20 years ago, the new military governments do not seek pure dictatorial rule. Moreover, the military are seriously interested in economic development and social advancement. There are influential officers in Latin America who believe the basic problems of their countries can be solved only through reforms implemented by the armed forces in the face of what they regard as the inability of civilian politicians to do the job.

The Roman Catholic Church has also marched onto the battlefield of social revolution. Once a main factor in preserving the status quo, it now resolutely advocates reform. In many countries the church has become a very progressive force—and this is one of the most significant events in Latin America.

It has been argued that all the new movements in Latin America are simply a response to the pressures unleashed by Castro's Communist take-over in Cuba. This is probably true as far as it goes, but it may be more accurate to say that while Castro's revolution has served its historical function, the great Latin-American trends have already submerged it and are now flooding out in new directions.

II The Present and the Future

I

Roads: The Missing Links

LATIN AMERICA's social revolution is not going to achieve the millennium right away. The average annual income of an inhabitant of Latin America stood in 1964 at the equivalent of $306, four dollars more than in 1960 just before the Alliance for Progress was launched. But even this slight gain is illusory. There are millions of Latin American's with annual incomes around $100, and if the area-wide average is about three times that figure it is because statisticians include the high petroleum revenues of Venezuela, which only recently have begun to seep down to the people of that land.

Let us look at $306 in terms of what it will buy in certain countries. In Venezuela, where things are costly, $306 a year corresponds to something like

1,200 bolivars annually, which is far from sufficient to purchase enough food for a family, let alone to procure adequate housing. In Brazil $306 a year is 540,000 cruzeiros at 1965's median exchange rate. This is below the government-decreed minimum wage for a worker and does not even begin to buy the food a family ought to have. Moreover, in the Brazilian northeast there are hundreds of thousands of people whose income is in the vicinity of 180,000 cruzeiros ($100) annually, which puts them in effect outside of the money economy. Similar income levels are to be found in the mountains of Bolivia, Peru and Ecuador, in several Central American republics and in Haiti.

The first time I became really aware of what an annual income of $100 can mean to a human being was in 1960, when I flew to Recife, Brazil, to write a series of articles on the northeast. On my first morning in Recife I decided to take a walk to see what the city was like. Leaving behind the modern apartment houses and office buildings of the downtown section, I found myself on a bridge near the mouth of a river that empties into the South Atlantic.

It was low tide and suddenly I realized that the river bed, as far as the eye could see, was crowded with men, women and children, knee-deep in water, extracting something from the muddy bottom. They were the crab-pickers, people whose only means of subsistence was the caranguejo crab they found in the river. The caranguejo provided the mainstay of their diet and what was left over could be sold—for the equivalent of less than a penny for a sack of crabs. And every day, at morning and evening low tide, they trooped by the thousands to the river for their caranguejos.

The Recife crab-pickers represent a small part of the surplus population of the rural areas, people who stream into the cities in search of work and housing. Recife alone has several hundred thousands of these migrants. Other cities in Brazil's northeast have additional hundreds of thousands. Rio de Janeiro and São Paulo, the country's metropolises, are the homes of more than a million slum dwellers. The slums grow in all the Latin-American cities as fast as the rural population increases each year, which means by the millions, because virtually no Latin-American nation has solved its agricultural problem.

What has emerged, instead, from the centuries of colonial rule and subsequent self-rule is a vast region of the world deficient in agriculture but now dotted with industrial complexes. Because the Latin-American countries long resented being chiefly producers of raw materials, a status forced upon them first by their European masters and then by their own leaders over the generations, a great effort was made after World War II to industrialize. Latin America's resources and capital obtained abroad were pumped into industrialization projects while the governments and economic elites disregarded the basic fact that an industrial society could not be built without the foundation of a food-producing farm economy.

The results were disastrous. On the one hand, the promise of industrial employment in the cities became a magnet, attracting the millions from the countryside—the migrants who now pick crabs in Recife, who crowd the hillside slums of Rio and Caracas and who live in poverty and squalor around cities like Lima, Santiago and Bogotá.

On the other hand, neglect of agriculture, including failure to change the nearly feudal land-tenure systems, lowered food-production levels at a time when the population explosion was creating millions of new mouths to feed every year.

Statistics published early in 1965 show that food production per capita dropped 1.6 per cent from 1954 to 1964 while the population was growing at an annual rate of more than 3 per cent. This has produced food shortages in the cities, where a measure of purchasing power does exist, and therefore a dangerous increase in inflation. In Chile, for example, the cost of living rose 86 per cent in a single year until it was partly arrested by severe control measures. In Brazil the rise topped 100 per cent in 1963 and was zooming toward the 150-per-cent mark in 1964 when a new revolutionary government stepped in with stern anti-inflationary policies.

Because wage increases cannot keep up with the rising prices, the average Latin-American worker or white-collar clerk is in debt. He owes money at a food store, at a bank or at the shops where he buys clothing, furniture or appliances.

The nation, too, becomes indebted. To meet rising costs of government operations, paper money is printed in cascades, adding to the inflation and further lessening the value of the currency. Staggering budget deficits are met by issuing more paper money as the vicious spiral of inflation continues.

Because, except in a few cases, exports of raw materials do not produce enough revenues to pay for imported products and industrial equipment and to finance economic development projects, nations acquire staggering foreign debts as well. Matters have reached the point where each time a Latin-American government contracts a new foreign loan, much of it has to be earmarked for repayment of previous loans.

To make matters even worse, the world prices of Latin America's export commodities are slumping. To take just two examples, sugar was fetching slightly over 2 cents a pound early in 1965, down from 11 cents a pound a year earlier, and coffee, which brought as much as 86 cents a pound in 1955, dropped heavily, climbing back to less than 40 cents in the first few months of 1965. Since sugar is an important source of income for at least six Latin-American nations and coffee is the main source of revenue for 15, the impact of this can be imagined.

Latin-American economists argue that it is impossible to plan rationally for the future when the most carefully prepared estimates of anticipated income can be rendered worthless in weeks or months by a change in overseas markets which Latin Americans cannot control. With the advent of the Alliance for Progress some provisions have been made to ease the shock of price declines, but they are at best stopgap measures.

Finally, all Latin America's economic problems are aggravated by geography. No country can develop properly so long as jungles and mountains isolate the seacoast from the backlands and the producing centers from their natural markets.

The United States can be crossed from the Atlantic to the Pacific by train or car in days. But an overland trip across South America may take weeks. Two antiquated railway systems provide the only surface links from ocean to ocean.

One is the Trans-Andean Railroad, running from Buenos Aires, Argentina, to Santiago, Chile, but it is closed from May to September, when the South American winter piles the snow high in the Andean pass. The second runs from Argentina or Brazil across the Bolivian highlands into Peru. A trip on it, however, is more of a safari than a train ride, as Lake Titicaca has to be crossed by boat and there is never any assurance of making connections on either the Bolivian or the Peruvian side. For transporting goods this link is virtually useless.

The only way to travel by automobile down the east coast and over to and up the west coast of South America is to drive from Bahia in the Brazilian northeast (the terminus of the only all-weather road) south to Rio de Janeiro, then to Buenos Aires, across the Andean pass in the summer (through the railroad tunnel) and up the west coast to Bogotá, Colombia, over the Pan-American Highway. The trip has been accomplished by determined motorists in weeks, but it has not occurred to anyone to ship goods by highway from Bahia, say, to Lima, Peru.

As for a real link between North and South America, even the Pan-American Highway does not provide that. There is a long break between northern Colombia and Panama City because nobody has ever tried to cut a road through the Darien Peninsula, reputed to have the thickest jungle in the world.

In short, transportation arteries among the Latin-American countries remain so primitive as to discourage any serious trade between them—and therefore to eliminate potential new markets. The situation is not much better within most of the republics, where roads for the most part do not constitute economic links.

Brazil, the giant of Latin America, has been working hard to build a highway network and today it is possible to drive and to transport goods along the lengthy coast and to some points in the interior. But the entire northern section of Brazil, the huge Amazonas region, is isolated from the rest of the country. A highway was cut in the late nineteen-fifties from the new Brazilian capital of Brasília, in the central plateau, to the port of Belém. But it was never paved and the jungle is rapidly reclaiming it. Manaus, the big port in the western Amazonas region, can be reached from the outside only by river or air. It is quietly stagnating in the humid heat along with all the Amazon River towns stretching from Belém to Iquitos in Peru.

In the mountainous countries like Peru, Bolivia, Chile and Ecuador there is often no overland travel between many population centers or else the journeys, sometimes on muleback, take days. The isolated communities produce only for their own consumption, taking no cognizance of the modern world.

If Latin America is ever to emerge from her underdeveloped state, steps must be taken to equip her with arterial and access roads so that each republic can become a real economic unit and the region as a whole can integrate economically.

It has been often said that Latin America is an area of contrasts and distortions. Compare, for instance, some of the teeming cities with the backward rural regions.

São Paulo and Mexico City are among the Western Hemisphere's most important industrial centers, catering to populations of three or four million and to the surrounding regions. In eight years the São Paulo automotive industry has become the world's ninth largest, turning out 200,000 units annually. Both São Paulo and Mexico City are plagued by awesome slums, but they have produced the backbone of Latin America's modern middle class. Provincial cities like Belo Horizonte in Brazil, Cali and Medellín in Colombia and Monterrey in Mexico are also significant manufacturing centers with an industrial middle class coexisting alongside destitute slum dwellers.

These and other modern or modernizing cities are the engines for a Latin-American economic breakthrough. But until a relationship develops between them and Latin America's rural vastnesses progress will remain stymied. The basic economic problems will not be solved, the improvement in over-all social conditions will not be attained and the Latin-American revolution will wind up in a dead end of frustration.

II

Man's Plight and Man's Hope

LATIN AMERICA's greatest potential asset is man. The extent of his skills, education, health and capacity for creative and productive work will determine whether Latin America breaks through into the 20th century or remains an overpopulated region of worsening stagnation.

Yet no other asset in Latin America has been as neglected as man. He is illiterate (close to 45 per cent of all Latin Americans cannot read or write) or semieducated and is rarely equipped with the skills required to participate in the technological age. His health is poor and his life expectancy is low. He is undernourished, if not frequently hungry. He is underemployed and often unemployed. He is ill-housed or not housed at all in the commonly accepted sense of the word. He is ill-clad.

"If we are going to build Latin America, we must first build, or at least repair, the Latin-American man," a famous sociologist once told me.

"How can you expect a man chronically ill and chronically undernourished to become a vibrant nation-builder?" he asked. "It is a vicious circle that must be broken or there will be no future for us."

And of course this vicious circle becomes more vicious as Latin America's population keeps growing at an ever-increasing rate. There is irony in this, for the concerted efforts of Latin-American governments to apply modern medical and sanitary techniques have accelerated the rate of population increase. Less infant mortality and a higher life expectancy mean ever more people. The net effect, therefore, is that Latin America must run faster and faster just to stand still in terms of over-all living standards.

However, economists and sociologists believe the vicious circle can be broken by massive measures aimed at social advancement and economic development.

The idea is that if the Latin-American man is given the minimal conditions of health, education and housing he will be equipped to handle efficiently and creatively the jobs being opened up by new government and private investments. Once he begins to produce he becomes a consumer. This in turn creates a demand for more goods and services and thus additional jobs. This is how a modern society is created, the economists say, and once the process is set in motion it proceeds automatically.

But, first, there is man and the woes that beset him. When the Alliance for Progress was formally launched at a conference in Punta del Este, Uruguay, in August, 1961, the principal social needs of Latin America were listed as health, housing, education, pure water and a fair land-tenure system.

Health, of course, is paramount, and it depends on proper nourishment, pure drinking water and decent housing. Let us start with nourishment. Statistics show that 11 of Latin America's 22 republics—including Brazil, the largest and most populous—produced less food per inhabitant in 1964 than they did 10 years before.

In 1964 the daily calorie intake per inhabitant in 14 Latin-American countries was below the 2,500 minimum required by many people for health and normal activity. In three countries it was below 2,000 calories. Yet there are even grimmer instances.

In many parts of Latin America rice and beans form the bulk of every meal, if not the whole meal, and a person may have to live on 720 calories a day. Coffee, which in many areas is the principal beverage, has zero calories. And aside from insufficient calories the average Latin-American diet is completely unbalanced.

Given this chronic state of undernourishment, it stands to reason that the Latin-American man tends to be listless and relatively unproductive, as well as highly vulnerable to various diseases.

In the Andean highlands the insufficiency of calories leads to the chewing of the coca leaf, a narcotic, but this in the long run destroys physical resistance. In the sugar-producing areas sugar cane is chewed for energy, but this brings about a dangerous imbalance in the diet.

To relieve the hunger and undernourishment— while long-term efforts are under way to improve farm production—the United States has been providing vast food shipments as loans or gifts from its agricultural surpluses. Emergency shipments have gone to the northeast of Brazil and to many other republics. Special programs are feeding 11 million schoolchildren throughout Latin America, often making the difference between a child's having the stamina to attend school and being forced to remain home because of substarvation.

The next health problem is water. Searching for Latin-American health statistics, I came upon a book by a former Brazilian health minister that had a cover photograph which illustrates this problem better than any treatise I have ever read.

The photograph showed a woman standing in a shallow stream washing a baby in a large wooden bowl. Behind her another woman was rinsing food in water from the same stagnant stream. This scene, repeated a million times a day, explains why gastritis, enteritis, schimatosis and other water-borne diseases are the first cause of death in at least six Latin-American countries and the second cause in at least three others. They are, moreover, the leading killers of infants in at least half the republics. In the Brazilian northeast, a vast area inhabited by 25 million people, half of all the babies die before the age of one because of schimatosis. In one township in 1959 not a single infant lived to see his first birthday.

Those who survive schimatosis in infancy or acquire it later in life are slowly destroyed by it. In children the symptoms are enormously distended bellies, almost fleshless limbs and unspeakable apathy. The sight of children in whom only the eyes seem alive is one of the most heartbreaking experiences of travel in the Brazilian northeast or the Central American lowlands.

The way to eradicate schimatosis and other gastric diseases is to provide pure water. The magnitude of the problem is illustrated by the fact that in 1963 only 10 per cent of Latin America's rural populations had access to pure water. Less than half the urban populations enjoyed municipal water systems and sewer services. Asunción, the capital of Paraguay, got a municipal water system only in 1960, and hundreds of other cities still do not have one. Although a major goal of the Alliance for Progress is to provide pure water through municipal systems in cities and well-drilling in rural areas, the rapid growth of the population tends to worsen the situation.

The dramatic benefits of pure water were demonstrated to me a few years ago when I visited a Peruvian highlands village where wells had been drilled as part of a community project financed by the Inter-American Development Bank. First there was the pride of the village elders, who led me to the wells as soon as I arrived. Then there was the enthusiasm of the regional public-health physician.

"You wouldn't believe it," he said, "but in the 18 months since the pure water system was installed gastric diseases have fallen off by more than one-half. And the kids are healthier, tougher and have the kind of joy of living that I haven't seen in a long time in these mountains."

There is, of course, a close relationship between health and general living conditions, particularly housing. And housing is one of Latin America's gravest problems. Unsanitary and crowded dwellings not only contribute to disease but also demean man and affect his attitude toward life.

The population explosion aggravates the situation. Present estimates put the housing shortage at 15 million dwelling units, half in the overcrowded cities. Since an average Latin-American family is calculated at five persons, this means that 75 million people lack even the most elementary type of adequate housing.

In addition, much of the so-called adequate housing that exists is in reality grossly inadequate, both in the cities and in the countryside. It has been estimated that to meet all Latin America's housing requirements at once would cost more than $23 billion, or 32 per cent of her annual gross product.

In the countryside a thatched-roof cottage with a door and a window is a luxury even though it may house 10 or more persons. In most areas there is no electricity, no running water, no sewers, not even outside sanitary facilities. Life begins when the sun rises and ends when night falls, for kerosene and candles, which could provide artificial light, cost too much.

There is yet worse to be found. There are huts of dry mud, windowless and with only a hole for an entrance. There are caves in the mountains inhabited by human beings and their animals alike.

When rural families migrate to the cities in search of jobs and a better existence, they trade their huts for urban slums that are like awful running sores. Depending on geography and topography, the slums occupy hillsides or develop in vast "belts of poverty" surrounding the cities.

In 1961 almost 40 per cent of the population of Rio de Janeiro, or close to 1.2 million people, lived in the *"favela"* slums of the city's hills. In 1961 in

Chile 14 per cent of the population of 8.5 million inhabited the slums around the major cities. No Latin-American metropolis is free of this cancer.

Nothing illustrates the housing problem better than the story of an American reporter who asked his cab driver one evening in a Central American city why so many people slept in doorways. The driver looked around, shrugged his shoulder and replied: "Because it is night, señor."

The life in slums and doorways breeds crime, promiscuity and a further breakdown of the social structure, all of which increases day by day as migrants keep streaming in from the desolate countryside. Again this emphasizes the urgency of a land reform that would keep the peasant population in the fields and give them a chance to earn a decent living.

There is a major effort under way, aided by the Alliance for Progress, to build low-cost housing, and in the first four years of the program much has been accomplished. But there are difficulties even in moving slum dwellers to modern housing equipped with sanitary facilities, electricity and other services.

The problem, of course, is the transition from one culture to another. I remember the time in Rio de Janeiro when the government moved several hundred families from their hillside slums to a brand-new community of concrete one-family houses. The old slums were burned, but within days it developed that the resettled families were renting their new houses to others and surreptitiously returning to the hills and rebuilding their shacks. The reason was that the sudden shift from slum to modern community destroyed what had become virtually tribal patterns of life and the slum dwellers felt lost in their new environment. When a housing development was built in Caracas, Venezuela, its new inhabitants wrecked the sanitary facilities and other installations with which they were not familiar and quickly turned the buildings into tenements. In recent years, therefore, the housing authorities in most cities have provided trained social workers to ease the cultural transition.

It is impossible to estimate the percentage of unemployed in Latin-American cities, but it is presumably very high. Paradoxically, because so many of the jobless are unskilled laborers, there exists in many industrial areas a shortage of trained workers, and in some cases these are drawn from abroad.

One reason why unemployment cannot be estimated is that so many people are underemployed or partly employed. They are the lottery-ticket vendors, the bootblacks and a whole galaxy of others who live by their wits, odd jobs or relief.

What are the remedies for Latin America's social ills? There are at least three, none of which will be easy to carry out and all of which must be undertaken.

The first is to solve the land problem through agricultural reforms and changes in the land-tenure patterns. An intensive and rational system of land cultivation—aided by rural credit and the construction of roads from farms to markets—would raise food production, give the people more to eat and encourage the peasants to remain in the countryside. When Venezuela began her gradual land-reform program in 1959 the effects were felt both in a marked increase in agricultural output and in the slowing down of migration to the cities.

Despite the commitments made at the Alliance for Progress conference in 1961, however, land reform has still to be put into effect in most of the republics. Mexico, Bolivia and Cuba carried out reforms as part of their respective revolutions, but elsewhere, with the exception of Venezuela, resistance remains formidable, though in some countries there is paper legislation or taxation designed to force landlords to sell their holdings to the state so these can be distributed among peasant families.

The gulf between the very rich and the very poor still tends to widen, mainly because of the population explosion, but many economists see the likelihood that this trend will gradually be reversed, and therein lies the second cure for Latin America's ailments.

This is rational economic and industrial development combined with expanded education, which would modernize the Latin-American republics and enlarge the new middle class.

In a short span of years this middle class has already become a powerful force and it exercises political control in a number of the more developed republics. Numerically it still constitutes a marked minority, but its impact on the new trends is great.

Because expanding industry in such centers as São Paulo, Mexico City, Caracas and Cali has been raising living standards for at least a section of the population, the middle class has visibly altered metropolitan patterns. Traffic jams are now commonplace in most major cities as more and more people become car-owners. Television sets are manufactured in a half-dozen countries to satisfy the growing demand. The days are gone when an electric refrigerator was such a status symbol that a family installed it in the living room so all visitors could see this proof of affluence. Today the TV set, stereo and the automobile have become the status symbols of the Latin-American middle class.

Walt W. Rostow, the economist who represents the United States on the steering committee of the Alliance for Progress, believes the key to Latin America's future is the creation of what he calls "national markets." A national market, he explains, would incorporate all the people of a country into the producing and consuming class, force a greater circulation of goods and money, and in time result in a vast expansion of the urban middle class and the establishment of a rural middle class. But here again the land problem must be solved first.

The third way to attack Latin America's social evils is to slow down the rate of population increase, through planned-parenthood measures or plain birth control.

Since Latin America is predominantly Roman Catholic, this seemed impossible only a few years ago. But the new attitude of the church on social problems in general and on limiting population growth in particular looms as one of the greatest of revolutionary changes.

The final attitude of the church awaits the over-all decisions on birth control to be reached at the 1965 session of the Vatican's Ecumenical Council. But for the first time overpopulation is being discussed openly by cardinals, bishops and parish priests. Church groups participate in the work of organizations studying population problems and planned-parenthood measures.

"We are beginning to tell our parishioners that a good Catholic does not raise a large family unless he can afford to feed, clothe and educate his children," a Latin-American bishop told me recently. "You would be surprised how much difference this has already made."

The Roman Catholic Church, in fact, now stands in the forefront of social-reform efforts in Latin

America. The Vatican's trend toward consecrating younger cardinals and bishops—and its recent encouragement of liberal priests—has profoundly altered the character of the church in many countries, notably Brazil, Chile, Bolivia and Peru.

The new cardinal in Lima, Peru, has been making speeches advocating social justice and land reform that have led some landowners to accuse him of Socialist or Communist sympathies. The bishops in the Brazilian northeast have organized their own "Peasant Leagues" for land reform to counteract the leagues formed by extreme leftists.

The problem of the Latin-American man—the social problem of Latin America—has barely begun to be solved. But for the first time, in the spread of the Latin-American revolution, there is hope for the future.

III

The Social-Minded Soldiers

As a long history of revolts and uprisings makes clear, Latin America is unstable. This instability stems from the weakness of her political systems. Because of the lag in mass education, the practice of politics has been traditionally restricted to extremely narrow groups. Literacy requirements in most of the republics still prevent as much as half the potential electorate from voting. Even in the countries where elections are held regularly, decision-making has long rested in the hands of tiny power groups.

In this century the main political contest has been between democratic systems and dictatorships. What is largely new today is that the dictatorships generally show or profess to show as much concern about economic and social problems as the democratic regimes do. Therefore the question being asked in Latin America now is whether progress can be better achieved under democratic or authoritarian governments.

Interestingly enough, the arguments for authoritarianism as the road to economic development and social justice come from both the extreme left and the extreme right—though for different reasons.

I remember a lengthy discussion on this point with Premier Fidel Castro in Havana in July, 1959, about six months after he won power with his revolution. Along with a fellow correspondent of *The Times*, I pressed him on whether he would hold the free elections he had promised during his guerrilla war against the dictatorship of Fulgencio Batista.

Castro was at first evasive—this was still the day when the Cuban revolution presented a liberal and democratic image to the world—but finally he took up the issue. My scribbled notes on the conversation (it was a long chat rather than an interview) show that he put it this way:

"You talk about elections and democracy, but the whole history of Latin America demonstrates that this democracy has been a farce. . . . How can you talk about democratic elections in which only minorities participate? . . . There can be no true democracy without social justice, without a social revolution, and the so-called democratic systems in Latin America will not allow social justice. . . . If

I called elections today I would win by an overwhelming margin. But to plunge Cuba today into an
election campaign would paralyze the process of social revolution. . . . We would have a congress
that would talk and talk, argue and argue, and in
the end there would be no social revolution left
. . . . The revolution has given us a mandate for
social change and we must carry it out ourselves. . . ."

Shortly thereafter Castro delivered a series of
speeches in which he asked Cubans: "Elections, for
what?" and proceeded to announce that the democracy already achieved under his revolution was pure
democracy. It was pure, he explained, because what
the revolutionary government was doing in terms of
agrarian reform and urban reform had the unanimous support of the nation as shown by the ap-
plause of the crowds. Subsequently an official slogan
was unveiled. "We've already elected Fidel!" it proclaimed.

Castro's argument that economic progress and
social justice could be better achieved without democracy and representative government has been
made before and since by many Latin-American
rulers, including those with little or no interest in
easing the lot of their people.

It was stated as far back as 1937 by the late Getúlio Vargas as he turned Brazil into a semifascist
dictatorship under the name of the "New State." Yet

Vargas was a serious reformer who gave Brazil her first taste of social legislation and he was for a quarter of a century the idol of the masses.

The argument for authoritarian rule in the name of social justice was likewise offered by the Argentine dictator Juan D. Perón. His regime, based on labor unions and the army, was an attempt of sorts at a social revolution, but it bogged down in scandals, corruption and ruinous economic policies. Yet 10 years after Perón's ouster in 1955 a great many Argentine voters still supported political parties pledged to *peronismo*.

The view that Latin Americans could not rule themselves and that politics serve only to distract them from the task of economic development was expounded to me in 1957 by a brilliantly educated but very cynical cabinet minister in the dictatorial Venezuelan regime of General Marcos Pérez Jiménez. Quoting Alexander Hamilton and Thorstein Veblen between sips of Scotch and soda in his magnificently decorated villa, he insisted that Venezuelans had to be governed by elites. "And, of course, we are the elite," he said.

After a revolution overthrew the Pérez Jiménez dictatorship in 1958 it turned out that the elite had not only squandered Venezuela's fabulous petroleum revenues but had also led the country into a debt of several billion dollars. During the period of that "elite" rule Venezuela's illiteracy rate had in-

creased and her food production had dropped cata-
strophically.

After the Cuban revolution and the Alliance for
Progress made social justice and economic development highly popular concepts, the notion again
emerged that they could best be achieved by authoritarian governments. This was employed as justifica-
tion for a series of military take-overs in the early
nineteen-sixties, though none of the new rulers was
candid enough to speak out frankly against the democratic process.

It has to be recognized, however, that the new
breed of military or military-backed regime takes
social and economic progress infinitely more seriously than did the dictatorships of the previous generation, such as that of Pérez Jiménez.

The Brazilian government of President Hum-
berto Castelo Branco, which came to power in
April, 1964, as the result of a military revolt that
deposed the constitutional regime of President João
Goulart, is repairing the nation's finances, empha-
sizing economic development and trying to move
ahead with blueprints for land reform. At the end of
its first year the Castelo Branco government could
not be described as a military dictatorship, though
the President is an army marshal who was chief of
staff, but neither could it be called a democracy. It
could best be termed a political halfway house. A
feature of the Latin-American scene in recent years,

this halfway house is a compromise between outright military rule and the maintenance of certain democratic aspects of government, including a commitment to hold free elections "as soon as possible" and restore full-fledged democracy.

The halfway house was erected in a number of Latin-American countries from the inception of the Alliance for Progress in 1961 to the end of 1964. Although circumstances varied in each case, the common denominator was a decision by the armed forces to assume power when mounting pressures for social change seemed to lead to chaos under the civilian government. The fear of Communist influence was cited in every instance to justify the takeover, though it almost never was a valid argument.

However, the difference between old-fashioned military rule in Latin America and the coups d'état by the armed forces in the nineteen-sixties is that the generals and colonels nowadays are not like most of their earlier counterparts, bent on preserving a conservative status quo. In fact, they often are the articulate advocates of social change, with the proviso that only the military are equipped to bring this about.

This attitude stems from the transformed character of the Latin-American military officer, and it has already led to talk about "Nasserism"—that is, the pattern developed by President Gamal Abdel Nasser in the United Arab Republic of granting to the military the power to supervise the dispensation of social justice.

Just as the Roman Catholic Church has been revising its views in Latin America, so have the armed forces, once the other pillar of the status quo. The key is the growing importance of the middle class.

Whereas the generals of a generation or two ago usually represented the closest thing to an aristocratic caste in Latin America, the modern officer is a product of the middle class in the broadest sense of the term. He probably comes from a middle-class family, his immediate relatives are middle class and he is exposed to the anxieties and problems of the middle class. He suffers, as his civilian relatives and friends do, from the inroads of inflation. Because he is better educated than his counterpart of a generation ago he is aware of the economic, social and political pressures around him and therefore responds to them. For the first time in Latin-American history the military officer is a full-fledged member of society as a whole rather than just of a separate clique.

This identity with the people began to assert itself in an important way in the nineteen-fifties during the cycle of antidictatorial revolts. In each case—in Argentina, Colombia and Venezuela—the officers' corps swung the armed forces against the military dictators when it became plain that popular opposition to them was widespread.

In Argentina it was a group of officers who

sparked the revolt against Perón, responding to the sentiments of the middle class and the students. I was in Córdoba, the inland city where the revolution broke out, when liberating troops mopped up the last points of Peronist resistance. Though bullets were still flying, thousands of Córdoba's inhabitants filled the streets to cheer and embrace the soldiers. Within three days all the army commands joined the revolution. That years later the Argentine workers showed a belated loyalty to Perón by supporting parties pledged to *peronismo* was due in large measure to the inability of democratic governments to move ahead with social reforms.

I was in Colombia in May, 1957, reporting for *The New York Times* the revolution against General Gustavo Rojas Pinilla, the vain and corrupt military dictator. Again the uprising began with student riots, followed by strikes in which the workers were supported by their employers. On the fourth day of the rebellion I asked a key army commander how long he thought the armed forces would back Rojas Pinilla. He winked, smiled and said: "One more good riot by the students and the others and we'll march to San Carlos Palace to tell the President he is finished."

He was as good as his word and four days later I stood nearby as he announced to a delirious crowd that "the army has joined the people" and the dictator had been deposed.

Not quite a year later much the same thing happened in Venezuela. First a group of air-force pilots who had been trained in the United States attempted to overthrow Pérez Jiménez by bombing his palace. They failed and fled to Colombia, where one of them said to me: "It was you Americans who taught me all about democracy when I was being trained in the States, so why don't you help us now to overthrow the dictator?"

A week later student riots broke out in Caracas. The students were joined by industrial workers, the middle class and the wealthy. The army remained loyal to Pérez Jiménez for three weeks; then one night a delegation from the armed forces arrived at Miraflores Palace to tell him he was out. The Caraqueños danced in the streets to celebrate the return to democracy.

In the ensuing years the military intervened in several countries. In 1962 they overthrew elected presidents in Argentina and Peru because the political situations were breaking down. But in both cases the armed forces supervised free elections a year later and at this writing the democratic regimes that resulted are gaining in strength.

In Ecuador the military ousted President Julio Arosemena, chiefly because of his propensity for alcoholic beverages, and has operated a benevolent authoritarianism, pushing ahead with development plans. A land-reform law was approved in 1964, abolishing *huasipungo,* or serfdom, and opening the way for the distribution of some land to the unspeakably poor peasants of the Andean sierra. In Ecuador the military regard themselves as the proper instrument for social reform.

In the Dominican Republic, which suffered 31 years of brutal dictatorship under the late Generalissimo Rafael Leonidas Trujillo Molina, democracy lasted exactly seven months. In September, 1962, the military overthrew President Juan Bosch, who had won an overwhelming majority in the country's first free elections since 1924.

Bosch, a novelist and political scientist, came to power as a social reformer, but he quickly bogged down in problems with the military, the unwieldy bureaucracy and his own political party. He was accused of tolerating Communist infiltration—a charge never proved. The collapse of his regime, however, was chiefly due to the weakness of the nation's political institutions in the face of pressures for profound changes after three decades of dictatorship.

A civilian junta was placed in power by the military to replace Bosch. The new president, Donald Reid Cabral, a middle-class anti-Trujillo revolutionary and an auto dealer in private life, proceeded to discipline the military and assert civilian authority. He allowed an opposition newspaper, of which he was part owner, to criticize his regime at will. He promised presidential elections for late 1965 and set about rebuilding the economy.

But on April 24, 1965, the Dominican Republic exploded with a fury that had no parallel even in her troubled history. A civilian-military rebellion, claiming to act in the name of a restoration of constitutional government, ousted the Reid Cabral junta. In the nearly five weeks of ensuing civil war thousands of Dominicans were killed and other thousands injured as the rebels fought "loyalist" troops. It took the landing of 22,000 United States troops and extraordinary efforts on the part of international diplomats to bring the civil war under some sort of control, though at this writing the Dominican crisis is still unresolved despite an apparent settlement reached in September.

The military took over in Honduras in 1962, when that small country had begun to move toward basic social reforms. Unfortunately it lapsed back into stagnation under its dictator, Colonel Oswaldo López Arellano.

An army coup in Guatemala, also in 1962, handed power to a military group that considers economic development its mission. The incipient "Nasserism" of the Latin-American military is in evidence here, and in two years the country has registered an improvement in economic activity and growth. Elections are promised for March, 1966.

The 1964 revolution in Brazil—the first time the

democratic process had been interrupted there in 19 years—was the result of vast mismanagement, bordering on chaos, under Goulart. In the 30 months of his presidency Brazil's dynamic economic expansion came to a standstill, inflation broke all records, extreme leftists were placed in positions of power and a breakdown of the whole national structure seemed imminent.

For three months after the revolution the avenging military purged Congress and the federal and state governments, but then the moderating influence of President Castelo Branco asserted itself. A quiet, self-taught intellectual who rose through the army ranks from private to marshal, Castelo Branco is deeply committed to a restoration of the democratic process. He has preserved the freedom of Brazil's criticism-prone press and accomplished more in terms of basic reforms in one year than Goulart did in over twice that time despite his self-proclaimed devotion to social justice.

In Bolivia the army overthrew the government of President Victor Paz Estenssoro in November, 1964, bringing to an end a revolutionary phase that began in 1952. The revolution's main accomplishments were a partly successful land reform, the nationalization of tin mines and a powerful thrust in the field of education. The ouster of Paz Estenssoro was due primarily to a breakdown in both his regime and his National Revolutionary Movement party, mounting official corruption and an erosion of popular support after 12 years of power.

The new military junta, however, is not planning to undo the land reform or other positive features of the 1952 revolution. A young army colonel, serving as minister of economy, sees the role of the military as not to stop the social revolution but "to put order into it." He believes the proper function of the Latin-American armed forces, since they are not likely to fight modern wars, is to direct economic and social progress. His own accomplishments include using the Bolivian army in "civic action" programs of roadbuilding and school construction. This, again, is a case of incipent "Nasserism."

It is impossible, on the whole, to define the Latin-American political systems. They are very much in transition and each nation is seeking a permanent form of expression.

Thus Argentina, Chile, Peru, Uruguay, Venezuela, Panama, El Salvador and Costa Rica have democratic systems that function well in most cases. In Mexico the ruling Party of Revolutionary Institutions virtually appoints presidents, and freedom of expression is subtly regulated. Since the 1957 revolution Colombia has her National Front system, under which the Liberal and Conservative parties alternate in power every four years.

Outright dictatorships exist in Paraguay and Haiti. In Paraguay, President Alfredo Stroessner, twice elected without a rival candidate, is beginning to dispense political freedom in minuscule quantities while concentrating on economic development. In Haiti a mystical and brutal dictator, François Duvalier, presides over the abject poverty of his terrorized people.

At this time of transition Latin America's political structures suffer from internal weaknesses, from inadequate and often corrupt administrations and from the inability of central governments to coordinate policies in far-flung provinces.

As a rule most Latin American regimes operate through vastly inflated and generally inefficient bureaucracies. Political patronage swells government payrolls, adds to budget deficits and creates red tape that impedes essential programs. A common sight in government offices is groups of employes engaged in make-work activities, sipping coffee or gossiping on the taxpayers' time. Many persons in official favor supplement their incomes through part-time government jobs. I recall an acquaintance in Brazil who used to send a boy to punch the clock for him in a government office and collect his pay; he himself never set foot there.

Corruption on almost every level of public administration remains commonplace. Bribes may range from hundreds of thousands of dollars for a government construction contract to the equivalent of a dollar bill for expediting paper work. A famous story concerns a cabinet minister in Venezuela's dictatorial regime of the nineteen-fifties who is said to have ejected a European contractor from his office with the cry: "Don't you ever dare come here with less than a quarter of a million dollars."

To end corruption has been a major aim of the Cuban revolution under Castro and the Brazilian revolution under Castelo Branco. Both appear to have been reasonably successful.

"Corruption is a feature of the culture of under-development," a Latin-American sociologist wrote recently. "When you remove the underemployment and instill a sense of pride in public service, you will have eliminated corruption."

In the continuing Latin-American revolution the basic institutions will have to be strengthened and even rebuilt if the republics to the south of us are to overcome the tradition of instability. To do this is one of the chief objectives of the emerging generation of politicians and policy-makers.

IV

A New Breed of Leaders

WHAT POLITICAL TRENDS are the new Latin-American generations likely to pioneer? The emphasis is on finding novel solutions to old problems. Since more than half of all Latin Americans today are below the age of 25, impatience is growing and so is the desire for experimentation.

In all probability Latin America will not become Communist, but neither will she choose outright capitalism. Militating against both are the discernible trends in all the main groups of society: the younger generation of civilian politicians, the new breed of technocrats moving into positions of power, the intellectuals, the nationalistic-minded military men and, last but not least, the Roman Catholic Church.

The debate over what Latin America should become and how this is to be achieved goes on everywhere: in the press, in books on politics and economics, in classrooms at ancient universities and brand-new colleges, in government offices, at labor-union meetings and students' bull sessions.

San Marcos University in Lima is one of the oldest institutions of higher learning in the Western Hemisphere. Founded in the days of the Spanish viceroys, it witnessed Peru's independence, the turbulence of the 19th century, the modern dictatorships, the revolts and coups d'état and finally a form of stabilization under democracy. It was here that former Vice President Nixon received in 1958 his foretaste of spittle and stones.

I went over to the old campus, just a few blocks from Plaza San Martín, where so many political rallies are held, the day after President Kennedy's assassination in November, 1963. A reporter in Latin America has to keep in touch with student groups to sense the new trends or sometimes to be sure he knows the date and place of the next riot, and over the years I had been a frequent visitor at San Marcos. This time I ran into an acquaintance, a young assistant professor of economics. With a few of his graduate students we went across the street for a beer and at first the talk was all about President Kennedy and how his tragic death had shocked the Peruvians.

Then one of the students said: "Well, Kennedy is dead, but our problems stay with us. Where do we go from here?"

"It's obvious," answered a second student, an extreme leftist advocating violent revolution. "We just have to go on making the Indian masses conscious of the need for the revolution and give them leadership. Then and only then can they be emancipated. We had to do it when Kennedy was alive—now it is even more important.

The first student disagreed. He was a member of President Fernando Belaúnde Terry's Popular Action party and did not believe in violence.

"Sure," he said, "we too want to emancipate the Indian masses and give them land and work and food and schools. But the way to do it is *not* to start a bloody revolution and turn everything upside down the way you red-hot revolutionaries propose. There *are* other ways."

What those other ways are—or could be—was expounded to me the same week by President Belaúnde. The Peruvian chief executive, a dynamic man of 50 in a gray flannel suit, sat in an office that was surrounded by the splendor of bygone days. Outside, soldiers in colorful 19th-century uniforms guarded the gates of the presidential palace. To reach Mr. Belaúnde one had to be ushered through a labyrinth of salons and reception rooms hung with dark oil paintings and filled, it seemed, with the ghosts of viceregal courtiers.

But the President's office was cluttered with symbols not of the past but of the future. A scale model of a housing development occupied one table, which seemed fitting since Mr. Belaúnde is an architect. On the walls and special stands there were maps of new highways planned by the government, production charts and all the paraphernalia of Latin America's modern obsession with economic development.

Peru is a particularly difficult nation to develop. There is the coastal desert, then the snow-capped Andes and finally the jungle country beyond the mountains. The Incas once knew how to irrigate the desert and today it boasts oases of lush greenery. But the great mass of the population—the Indians and the half-caste *Cholos*—lives in the Andes, where sometimes it is harder to make a plant grow than in the desert. The jungle country is barely populated, though that is where much of Peru's oil reserves lie. This hostile geography is Peru's central problem.

However, President Belaúnde, as he explained it to me striding from map to chart in his office, believes it can be solved. The desert, the Andes and the jungle, he said, must be crisscrossed with penetration roads. Then the Indians and the *Cholos,* instead of crowding the high plateau cities and adding to the coastal cities' slums, could move out into the fertile jungle lands, clear them and colonize them.

This, Mr. Belaúnde declared, would begin to solve the age-old Indian problem, incorporate the Indians into modern society and help overcome the food-supply difficulties.

Much of what President Belaúnde outlined in 1963 is already taking place in Peru. Under a system of self-help, local populations are building the roads and conquering the new land, using tools supplied by the government. The army's engineers help out with bulldozers. The long-silent Andes and the forgotten jungle are coming alive.

What is happening in Peru illustrates the point that whenever a *positive* alternative is offered to a Latin-American nation, the danger of radical or totalitarian influence diminishes in proportion. The new generation of leaders understands this, and events have demonstrated that the threat of Castro's "exporting" his Communist-type revolution dwindles when efforts are made in a country to eliminate conditions that breed revolt.

The stories of Venezuela and Chile in 1963 and 1964 are good examples.

In Venezuela, beginning in 1961, extreme leftist groups tried to bring about the ouster of the Rómulo Betancourt government. President Betancourt had been elected in 1958 after the overthrow of the Pérez Jiménez dictatorship. The main reason he became the target of the extreme leftists, who were en-

couraged and aided by Cuba, is that his regime undertook to offer peaceful evolution as an alternative
to Castro's violent revolution. As a democratic reformer, Betancourt was thus a far more formidable
rival of Castro than government chiefs elsewhere
who talked of reform without doing much about it.
In short, Betancourt, who started a land-reform
program before Castro did, was in effect undercut-
ting the Cuban Premier's position as the prophet of
the Latin-American revolution for social justice.

The instrument fashioned by the leftists to dispose
of Betancourt was the FALN, a military organization whose initials in Spanish stand for Armed
Forces of National Liberation. The FALN was a
strange blend of people and ideas. Among its leaders were top men of the Venezuelan Communist
party and the even more radical MIR, the Movement of the Revolutionary Left. The leadership also
contained leftist military officers and disgruntled
rightist officers whom Betancourt had punished for
earlier attempts at revolt. The "troops," often re-
cruited by Marxist university professors, were even
more interesting. Some were idealistic and romantic
students who believed a revolution was urgently required. Others were youths who felt guilty and re-
bellious because their parents were wealthy and in
many cases had profited by the corruption of the
Pérez Jiménez dictatorship. Still others were young

right-wing extremists who hated Betancourt because his party had been instrumental in ousting the dictator.

The FALN "army" was well organized and hardhitting. Its members had courage and imagination. They hijacked planes in flight and a ship on the high seas. They blew up oil-transmission lines, attacked small military posts and kidnapped celebrities to call attention to their fight. Much of FALN's activity, which ranged from terrorism in the cities to attempts to establish guerrillas in the mountains, was patterned on Castro's earlier operations in Cuba. The Venezuelan revolutionaries assumed their movement would triumph because Castro's had succeeded.

But, as history promptly demonstrated, they were wrong. Conditions were different. In Cuba Castro had mobilized virtually the entire nation behind him in struggling against the dictatorship of Fulgencio Batista. In Venezuela the FALN was seeking to overthrow a government that was constitutional and democratic and also busily engaged in economic development and social improvement.

By late 1963 the FALN realized that if it was to win it had to prevent at all costs the presidential elections scheduled for December 1. The khaki-clad terrorists stepped up their attacks and threatened the voters with death if they dared go to the polls.

I visited Caracas, Venezuela's capital, shortly before the elections, just as the FALN terrorism was reaching its peak. There was nervousness in the city but no real worry. I had breakfast one morning with President Betancourt and found him much more concerned with food-production statistics than with the FALN. But then Betancourt was an unusually nerveless individual. Three years earlier he had barely escaped death when a radio-controlled car filled with dynamite was hurtled against his limousine. In the attack, engineered by the late Generalissimo Trujillo, then the Dominican Republic's dictator, President Betancourt suffered serious burns and for months could not use his hands. There were subsequent assassination plots against him, but apparently nothing could shake this rotund, bespectacled man, always puffing on his pipe and working on his development plans.

Raúl Leoni, the presidential candidate of Mr. Betancourt's party, was equally unruffled. One day we had lunch together in a steak house on a busy Caracas street. Only one bodyguard lounged nearby, despite a spate of terrorist attacks the night before. As we drank coffee, Leoni told me casually that the Venezuelan army had discovered the previous day a huge cache of Cuban arms smuggled in for the FALN. It was this shipment that led the Organization of American States to order sanctions against Cuba the following year.

The climax of the FALN story came December 1,

1963. Ignoring FALN threats, over 90 per cent of the registered voters went to the polls, electing Leoni President. It was clearly a mandate for continuation of the democratic social revolution through peaceful means.

Communism and extremism were again defeated a year later, this time in Chile. But there it was purely a political operation. In the September, 1964, presidential elections, Senator Eduardo Frei Montalva, a Christian Democrat, was opposed by Senator Salvador Allende, a Marxist backed by FRAP, the Socialist-Communist bloc. Their contest was of extraordinary importance because for the first time in the Western Hemisphere the possibility had arisen that a Marxist regime might be voted into office. It was evident that the outcome of the Chilean elections would have immense implications for the whole political future of Latin America, the fate of the Alliance for Progress and the entire relationship between Latin America and the United States.

Allende, who, like Frei, had tried for the presidency in 1958, was campaigning on a platform calling for nationalization of the American-owned copper companies, radical land reform and other measures that he said would bring social justice to Chile.

Frei's campaign was based on his slogan of "Revolution with Liberty." This signified that he too favored land reform and other progressive measures but was committed to maintaining democracy and averting the loss of liberty that had occurred in Cuba. Allende, an admirer of Castro, had frequently visited Havana, and the electorate assumed that if he won, Chile would become another Cuba.

In the end Frei obtained a smashing majority. His victory was interpreted primarily as a defeat for Marxism or Castroism. But later, in the congressional elections of March, 1965, when President Frei in effect submitted his program to a referendum, he scored an even greater triumph. This time it meant that the Chileans were determined to see their government move ahead with a vast and comprehensive program of reforms and economic development. It was as it had been with Belaúnde in Peru and Leoni in Venezuela, except more so.

One of the interesting things about President Frei —and this is true of all the new-breed leaders in Latin America—is that he is *not* flamboyant, *not* a demagogue, *not* even a great orator. To those accustomed to the pyrotechnics of Latin-American politics, to say nothing of the mesmerism of the bearded Fidel Castro, Mr. Frei is an almost improbable figure.

I first met him in 1956, when I began covering Latin America for *The Times*. He appeared for tea at a Santiago hotel, wearing brown tweeds, a furled umbrella over his arm. There was something quite professorial about him and the manner in which he discussed Chile's problems and how he would solve them. Quietly but with steely authority he talked of the need for land reform—and this was in the days before either Castro or the Alliance for Progress had made it the rallying cry it is now.

We met often after that teatime conversation and I counted on Mr. Frei to help me understand and explain in print the profound changes taking place in Chile and throughout Latin America. Since Mr. Frei always thought in hemispheric as well as Chilean terms, it was inevitable that after his election to the presidency he would immediately become a major hemispheric leader.

It is significant that Frei and his counterparts are the antithesis of the classical dictator—Perón, Batista, Rojas Pinilla, Pérez Jiménez and Castro. Frei is the strong-minded professor. Peru's Belaúnde is the restless architect, though his political history does include a few duels and a swim to freedom from an island prison. Venezuela's Leoni is the labor leader turned politician. President Arturo Illia of Argentina is a small-town physician. Marshal Castelo Branco in Brazil is a self-taught intellectual.

As a group, these men typify the new Latin America, the post-Castro Latin America. They believe in nonviolent "Revolution with Liberty." They have a great deal in common. For one thing, because of their origins, backgrounds and connections, they all represent the middle class. For another, all are strongly devoted to economic development and have provided the political framework for the emergence in recent years of the new class of Latin-American "technocrats"—the young planners, engineers, agrarian-reform specialists and businessmen. It is this class that has the task of transforming Latin America.

In sum, then, what this new breed of Latin-American presidents is giving the nations and the hemisphere as a whole is a sense of political stability that stems from economic and social progress. This is the best antidote to extremist revolutions.

If we are to accept the notion that much or most of Latin America is finally beginning to move toward a form of stability it has never known before, the question arises as to what political forms are likely to emerge.

If the present trends continue, one may risk the prediction that Latin America's development will be along left-of-center lines. Thus, in the Chilean, Peruvian and Venezuelan elections the chief contests were between left-of-center parties. Argentina was moving to the left of center even under Perón. Mexico has a tradition of leftist politics.

What does left-of-center development mean? Again, if recent trends are a guide, it implies economies based on the state's collaboration with private enterprise, domestic and foreign. Capitalism, even as it exists in the United States, does not seem suitable for countries as underdeveloped as those of Latin America. The area's planners and politicians argue that it is the role and responsibility of government to create the basic conditions in which private enterprise can flourish. They doubt, by and large, that private capital can assure the over-all economic development of Latin America. They contend that since private capital obviously will not build roads, schools or hospitals, the state's role must be considerable and the state must exercise control.

Latin Americans resent criticism from those in the United States who cry that this blend of government-run economies and private enterprise is a form of socialism. A Brazilian economist became quite angry one day as we discussed the problem.

"Why do Americans always take this holier-than-thou attitude?" he asked. "What is the real difference between what we are trying to do and what you have done?

"You have the Tennessee Valley Authority and Hoover Dam, but you criticize us for letting the state take over the power resources. Your labor unions can tie up the whole country overnight, but when we have a strike you cry 'Communism!' Your Securities and Exchange Commission, the Federal Reserve and all the regulatory agencies have more power over the United States economy and its private sector than almost anything ever devised or planned in Latin America. So, are *we* the socialists?"

On another level it is quite likely that Latin

America will seek growing independence from the United States in foreign policy. Her strong nationalism may in time lead her to join the uncommitted "Third World," though this does not necessarily imply anti-American sentiments and policies.

What is happening is that Latin America is becoming increasingly aware of her need for political and economic unity to deal with the industrialized nations and various economic blocs. The current talk of a Latin-American common market is a modern manifestation of Bolívar's dream of union.

Latin America also feels an identity with the underdeveloped countries of Africa and Asia and is likely to work with them on worldwide trade policies, as she did at the 1964 Geneva economic conference. The new Latin-American governments oppose Communism at home, but are interested in ties with the Communist world for the benefits they think may be derived. Thus, much of Argentina's foreign exchange comes nowadays from selling wheat to Communist China and the Soviet Union. Brazil's military revolution of 1964 purged extreme leftists, but the new regime is increasing trade with the Communist bloc. President Frei's first step in foreign policy was to establish diplomatic relations with the Soviet Union and the Eastern European states.

"We don't want to be like you, we want to be ourselves," a student leader at the University of São

Paulo told me recently.

"To you Americans democracy is equivalent to capitalism," said a Christian Democratic senator in Chile. "To us political democracy does not necessarily have to be capitalism. We must find our own form."

A Brazilian bishop, an energetic proponent of social reform in his native northeast, put it even more startlingly.

"We think that capitalism is un-Christian," he said. "The Christian way is cooperation, not competition for profit."

These, then, are the attitudes shaping the Latin-American revolution of the nineteen-sixties. The revolution, of course, is self-perpetuating. The more schools built, the more people become educated and the more ideas circulate.

And finally there is the most extraordinary of all elements of the revolution: the tiny transistor radio. Before its advent the massive illiteracy in Latin America paralyzed the flow of ideas, and vast regions were barely at the margin of political life. But today the transistor radio (usually imported from Japan and sold cheaply) is everywhere—in the Argentine pampas, the Bolivian Andes, the parched Brazilian northeast, the dusty towns of Central America, the islands of the Caribbean.

To peasant and slum dweller it brings radio courses in literacy and also propaganda broadcasts.

It brings the pronouncements of presidents and their political opponents. It brings the Voice of America and blandishments from Havana, Peking and Moscow in an unabating battle for the control of the Latin-American revolution.

III Latin America and the World

I

East versus West

LATIN AMERICA has acquired tremendous importance in world affairs in the last decade. Before that it was not uncommon for the people of the United States to take the vast area to the south of us for granted. When President Truman traveled to Rio de Janeiro in 1947, he told the Latin-American leaders clamoring for financial aid that war-ravaged Western Europe's needs had to come first. When Secretary of State John Foster Dulles attended a conference in Venezuela in 1954, he informed the Latin Americans that now it was Asia that held the priority for United States assistance and attention.

The Latin Americans, beset by their economic and political problems and beginning to realize their potential importance, deemed both the help and the attention of the United States vital. They needed the help to break the shackles of underdevelopment and they required the attention to overcome the feeling that they were the forgotten poor relations of the powerful West.

One day in 1956 I visited one of Latin America's leading statesmen, Oswaldo Aranha, Brazil's Foreign Minister and Finance Minister on many occasions and in 1948 President of the United Nations General Assembly. We sat in his home in Rio de Janeiro drinking coffee and discussing relations between the United States and Latin America.

"You know," Mr. Aranha said, "We Latin Americans are like a woman; we want and we need the money, but we also crave attention and so we want flowers too."

Both the money and the flowers finally started to arrive in 1961, when President Kennedy launched the Alliance for Progress. But Mr. Aranha did not live to see this. He died the year before, just as Latin America began to change from a safe "backyard" of the United States to a cold-war battlefield.

It was Cuba that brought the cold war to the Western Hemisphere when Castro allied his revolutionary regime with the Soviet Union and other Communist countries. Early in 1960 Castro decided that his future was with Moscow, not Washington. There are many theories as to why he chose Communism, and it may be useful to recount here his own version.

He gave it to me in June, 1961. The improbable setting for our extraordinary conversation was the big bar of the Hotel Riviera in Havana. I had gone to the Cuban capital to report the initial negotiations for the release of the prisoners taken in the Bay of Pigs invasion two months earlier. Castro, of course, had crushed that assault by U.S.-backed Cuban exiles who had sought to topple him.

The Cuban leader had just finished meeting with a delegation from Washington when I ran into him in the lobby of the hotel. I had not seen him for more than a year and he agreed to sit down for a chat. We went to the bar, ordered soft drinks, took them to a table and presently were joined by other newsmen, friends of Castro and even passers-by. Havana is very informal, so is Castro, and our chat soon became something of a public event. Khaki-clad girls with submachine guns, waiters, bearded soldiers, foreign visitors—just about everybody in the hotel seemed to gather around us, smiling, nodding, occasionally applauding.

We talked about the Bay of Pigs invasion, how Castro had planned his successful defense and what he would have done had he commanded the invaders. Then I asked him why he had chosen socialism or Communism as the ideology for his revolution and why he had allied himself with Moscow. Castro answered with a torrent of words, but I was able to take enough notes to retain the essentials of his explanation.

"I chose socialism because I have evolved politically," he said. "This is the only system, I became convinced, that can help Cuba develop economically and assure social justice for all the Cubans. . . . Why am I allied, as you call it, with the Russians? Well, it's very simple. When we started our revolution you Americans became hostile to us. You started economic reprisals, you took away our sugar quota and now you mounted this invasion of mercenaries. . . . And who helped us? Who took our sugar? Who gave us credits? Who helped us to arm ourselves? It was the Soviet Union . . . so are you surprised that *they* are our allies?"

Castro was oversimplifying, of course. He signed his first major economic and aid agreement with the Soviet Union in February, 1960, long before the United States initiated its reprisals and before it stopped its purchases of Cuban sugar. Nikita S. Khrushchev, then the Soviet Premier, promised Castro the protection of Soviet missiles in July, 1960, almost a year before the Bay of Pigs invasion. Cuban fliers went to Communist Czechoslovakia for training in handling jet fighters early in 1960. Soviet technicians and military advisers began streaming into Cuba about the same time.

So, whatever the reasons, the Soviet presence in Cuba was established early in 1960, sucking that Caribbean island and the rest of Latin America into the cold war. The United States began to consider Cuba and all Latin America in terms of the East-West struggle. Then came the Cuban missile crisis of October, 1962.

But even before that, Castro's Cuba had settled into her pattern of "socialist revolution," or Communist dictatorship.

In the name of the revolution and social justice, of which Castro spoke so often, the island was turned into a coldly efficient police state. Operating on the principle that "if you are not with us, you are against us," the regime built up an extensive secret police network backed by neighborhood, farm and factory "Committees for the Defense of the Revolution." Enemies and suspected enemies were arrested and often imprisoned without trial for lengthy periods. Revolutionary tribunals passed death sentences at the *paredón*—the execution wall.

Close to a quarter of a million Cubans—including many of Castro's early associates—fled their homeland to exile abroad. Subsequent purges further thinned out the ranks of these early supporters of the revolution and replaced them in the government with "reliable" Fidelistas. The press, radio and television offered nothing but carefully doctored official propaganda. Freedom was thus lost in Cuba, sacrificed to the elusive notions of a social justice that even after years of the revolution Castro could not quite bring about despite massive aid from the Communist countries.

It is still unclear what actually led to the installation in Cuba of Soviet missiles capable of hitting the United States—whether Castro requested them as protection against Washington or whether Khrushchev forced them on Castro in a gamble designed to confront the United States with nuclear blackmail. Castro has been quoted as saying that he asked for the missiles; the Russians have not said anything publicly.

In any event, the discovery by American surveillance aircraft of the Soviet missile emplacements on October 14, 1962, set the stage for the most dangerous crisis since the end of World War II—a crisis centered in Latin America. The world became fully aware of it a week later when President Kennedy announced in a broadcast speech that the missiles had been spotted and that the United States would use all necessary means to force their withdrawal.

Washington requested an urgent meeting of the Council of the Organization of American States to approve a United States plan for a naval and air blockade of Cuba. Preventing the shipment of more Soviet missiles and getting those already in Cuba out was a matter for the whole Western Hemisphere, the United States argued. President Kennedy in his speech had reminded the Latin Americans that their cities as far south and west as Lima, Peru, were within range of the Cuba-based missiles.

The Council met on the afternoon of Tuesday, October 22. The tension was terrific in the wood-paneled meeting room in the Pan American Union building just two blocks from the White House. President Kennedy and his advisers had finished drafting the proclamation of the blockade and were awaiting word of the Council's action to issue it.

It was vital that the Latin Americans act without delay so the process of forcing Moscow to withdraw its missiles could be set in motion. But a conference on the Alliance for Progress was being held in Mexico City that same week and it was not until mid-afternoon on Tuesday—18 hours after President Kennedy's speech—that the Latin-American ambassadors to the O.A.S. and the organization's top officials were able to reach Washington.

To make sure they had their instructions to vote for authorizing the blockade, the State Department had gone to extraordinary lengths. The night before, as President Kennedy was delivering his speech, the United States ambassadors in all the Latin-American capitals called on the presidents and foreign ministers to deliver copies of the resolution to be voted upon by the O.A.S. Because the President of Mexico happened to be flying from the Philippines to Hawaii, the text of the resolution was radioed to him aboard his plane.

But as the O.A.S. Council meeting was being called shortly before 4:00 P.M. it turned out that, despite all efforts, the Bolivian and Uruguayan ambassadors had not yet received their instructions. The two-thirds majority necessary to approve the blockade resolution was already assured, but the United States was shooting for unanimity so the Western Hemisphere would present a solid front to the world. A State Department official arranged for open telephone lines from the Council room to Montevideo, Uruguay, and La Paz, Bolivia, to enable the two ambassadors to receive their instructions in time. A third line was kept open to the White House.

The Uruguayan delegate never received his orders, for Uruguay is governed by a nine-man presidential council and the group could not agree at short notice what to do. He abstained. The Bolivian Ambassador's phone connection to La Paz was so bad that he could not hear his Foreign Minister, but he took matters in his own hands and voted on his personal authority for the resolution. No sooner had the vote—19 in favor and one abstention—been announced than an excited official advised the White House that the way was now cleared to declare the blockade. This was promptly done.

The action by the Latin Americans in support of the United States was the real opening move in the perilous week-long confrontation that led to Moscow's agreement to remove the missiles.

Two weeks later I found myself in a Navy plane off Cuba, observing the withdrawal of the missiles. The period between that hectically tense afternoon at the O.A.S. Council room in Washington and the peaceful, sunny morning over the Caribbean seemed to have been telescoped into minutes. Now I was standing in the open cargo door of a Navy transport, strapped to the metal clamps, as the pilot banked at 500 feet over a Soviet freighter carrying some of the missiles on deck. The Russian crewmen waved at us as they took off the heavy tarpaulin covering the missiles so we could check that they were really being shipped back to the Soviet Union. I remember a girl in a yellow dress standing amidships and waving, too. If there was anything completely incongruous in that crisis, it was the sight of the girl in the yellow dress, halfway between two lethal missiles, waving at an American plane coming out of the morning sun.

The pull-back of the missiles, though removing a grave threat to peace, did not end the cold war in the Western Hemisphere. Both Moscow and Havana continued their machinations in Latin America. There was the episode of the Cuban weapons landed a year later in Venezuela for the FALN guerrillas, and there have been other efforts by the Communists to gain ascendancy. Despite the splits within the

Latin-American Communist parties as a result of
the Moscow-Peking rift, these efforts go on everywhere in various guises, for the lands to the south of
us constitute one of the world's great prizes.

The possibility of Cuban involvement in the Dominican civil war in April and May, 1965, brought
again to the fore the question of Havana-inspired
subversion. With the support given the rebellion by
the three Communist factions in the Dominican Republic, the Johnson Administration feared that Castro's followers might in time capture the antidictatorial revolution. This in large part led to the landing
of American troops in Santo Domingo. It has been
argued that the fear was groundless, that the Communists never had a chance to take over the revolution, but it would have been folly to expect that Castro would remain indifferent to violence and chaos
so near Cuba. Whatever the final judgment, the fact
remains that inevitably Castro cast his shadow over
the Dominican revolution.

Latin America, a vast area with a rapidly expanding population, may become before the end of the
century a single great economic entity, particularly
if development plans are strenuously pushed and a
proposed common market goes into effect in the
nineteen-seventies. As such Latin-America is a potentially fabulous purchaser of products from the
United States, Western Europe, Japan and the
Communist countries. She also is an immense

source of raw materials, ranging from coffee to iron ore and petroleum, and before long Latin-American consumer goods may compete throughout the world with those of the traditionally industrialized nations. It is no wonder that East and West are now competing for Latin America's allegiance.

But, as we have noted before, tendencies gradually emerging in the region suggest that sooner or later it will incline toward the "Third World" concept of nonalignment in the cold war. Many of the new Latin-American leaders increasingly view the world as divided not between East and West, or democracy and Communism, but between underdeveloped and affluent lands. They feel that their future lies not primarily with either power bloc but with the relatively poorer countries that are seeking to become relatively richer.

II

A Tale of Two Cities

FOR A LONG TIME after she won independence Latin
America tended to look inward rather than out at
the world. In the first half of the 19th century the
Paraguayan dictator José Gaspar Rodríguez Francia, known as El Supremo, actually sealed off his
country's borders to prevent any contact with foreigners.

The world, of course, responded in kind.
Though hordes of misery-struck people from southern and eastern Europe emigrated to Latin America, they did so in general only if it were not possible
or feasible to enter the United States. And to London, Paris or Brussels, Latin America was little
more than an interesting investment area for big and
quick profits or a source of raw materials. Take

Manaus, for example.

Manaus is a Brazilian city on the Rio Negro near its confluence with the Amazon. Until the late 19th century it was just a steamy and mosquito-ridden river town almost in the center of the impenetrable jungle. And then rubber was discovered in the Amazon region. The *Hevea amazonica* tree spurted a white viscous liquid when its bark was slashed. That liquid was latex. Baked, it became rubber.

Latex brought a fortune to the jungle and Manaus became the improbably opulent capital of a rubber empire. In the years before World War I superb mansions rose and an opera house was erected with real gold leaf. Luxury liners sailed from England and the United States to the mouth of the Amazon and then upriver to Manaus. This fantastic jungle metropolis demanded and got the best in the world. It is said that Caruso and Gigli sang at the opera house and Pavlova danced.

Then suddenly the bubble burst. Brazilians insist an Englishman stole a rubber-tree cutting and took it to Malaya to start a plantation there. Whether this is true or not, the Amazon rubber boom collapsed and Malaya replaced Brazil as the world's foremost producer. By the middle of the nineteen-twenties the wealth, fame and glory of Manaus were gone.

In 1958 I visited Manaus and found it a quietly destitute city trying to maintain its pride. The broad tree-lined avenues were imposing but empty. Today a modern airport terminal and a new hotel with an air-conditioned bar are symbols of the Amazon region's never ending hope that if the rubber boom does not return, petroleum—or something—will be discovered. Geological surveys suggest that oil may be found, but so far not a single well is producing commercially.

My first stop in Manaus was the opera house. The gold leaf had long since vanished from the roof. Windows were broken. The name of some forgotten office-seeker in some old election was painted in huge red letters on the stone façade. I went inside and found the custodian, a wrinkled old man, dozing in his office. I wakened him and he showed me around. The frescoes on the ceiling had peeled off. A big cat sprang from the dilapidated box seats, once plush-covered, and hissed at us. The boards of the stage were broken and some were missing.

"Ever heard of Pavlova?" the custodian asked. "Well, she danced here once. That was a long time ago."

I left the cool mustiness of the opera house and went out into the blinding noon sun, away from the haunting memories of a prima ballerina pirouetting on the banks of a jungle river. Outside were the big black crowlike birds of Manaus. They were everywhere, on fences and roofs, shuffling on the pavement, circling low overhead, as if waiting for their daily share of the decay.

In the nineteen-fifties Dr. Juscelino Kubitschek, then President of Brazil, decided that the isolation of the Amazon region must end. It was a part of his grandiose plan to develop Brazil's economy and transform his vast country into a world power. Taking office in 1956, Kubitschek, a physician turned politician, attracted foreign investments to the tune of hundreds of millions of dollars. In the five years of his administration the São Paulo area became Latin America's biggest and most diversified industrial complex.

But Kubitschek had still other ideas and none was more daring than to build a new capital of Brazil in the empty central plateau in the State of Goiás. The new capital, to be called Brasília, was to be the hub of a wheel from which highways would radiate like spokes in all directions: to the Amazon region in the north, to the western jungles, to the industrial east and to the farm belt of the south.

Brasília, Kubitschek declared, would become the center not only of Brazil but of all Latin America. It would capture the attention of the world and bring more and more tourists and new investors.

In December, 1956, I flew with the President aboard a Brazilian Air Force C-47 from Rio de Janeiro to a grass landing strip in Goiás. All we found there was a two-story wooden structure that served as a guest house and as headquarters for a small group of young architects and engineers. We had lunch at a long wooden table, the plates of beans and rice atop blueprints, the knives and forks next to slide rules and pencils. Then a jeep pulled up and Kubitschek beckoned me to come along.

We drove to a knoll overlooking the prairie and savanna. Kubitschek jumped out of the jeep and pointed to a line of white pennants stretching ahead of us.

"See?" he said. "This is the presidential palace. . . . And you see the pennants there in the distance? That is the Congress . . . and there is the Supreme Court. . . ."

I remember nodding politely. Now as I look through my old notebooks I find an enormous question mark next to a scribble saying: "White pennants are the palace, JK says."

By 1961 all doubt had ended. Today where the pennants fluttered there stands the spectacular marble Palace of the Dawn. Down the wide main avenue are the Hall of Congress, the Supreme Court, the ministry buildings. To each side rise apartment houses and one-family homes. Kubitschek's vision had become reality and a city was born in the middle of nowhere. The future will tell whether Brasília can really become a functioning capital—in 1965 most government business was still being transacted in Rio—but there is no disputing the impact Brasília has made on the world. People everywhere have heard of the gleaming metropolis. And if Bra-

sília has not yet become the highway hub Kubitschek hoped it would, that too may be achieved some
day.

Manaus, then, may be said to symbolize the old
Latin America of boom and bust while Brasília
symbolizes the new Latin America bent on economic development, determined to make her mark
on the world and dedicated to attaining a measure
of security in the international marketplace.

This new outward look began at the end of World
War II with the creation of the United Nations. The
Latin Americans started out by being very important. They represented 20 votes in the General Assembly, or close to half the membership at the time
the United Nations Charter was signed in San Francisco in 1945. But with the growth of the U.N., particularly through the influx of new and underdeveloped African and Asian states, the importance of
Latin America in terms of votes diminished greatly
and the Latin Americans realized that their strength
lay in allying themselves with the rest of the underdeveloped world. They sought to increase trade with
both the capitalist West and the Communist East,
but at the same time they drew away from the great
industrialized countries, be it the United States or
the Soviet Union. The stirrings of neutralism began
to be felt in Latin America and the prices of primary
commodities became an overwhelming concern.

In 1964 the Latin-American republics joined

forces with the African and Asian lands in open opposition to the industrialized nations at the Geneva Conference on Trade and Development. They demanded price guarantees, preferential treatment and a whole series of measures designed to spur their economic progress. The conference gave birth to the so-called Group of 77, a bloc of underdeveloped countries. It was possibly a turning point in postwar history and certainly a milestone in Latin America's active participation in world affairs.

Not long ago I talked with an outstanding Chilean economist, a member of President Frei's team, about Latin America's new international role.

"Look here," he said. "You must forget the idea that we have to make a choice between the East and the West in the cold war. This is no longer the issue. Sure, we belong to the Western tradition and instinctively we are with the West. But the real choice we must face is whether we are prepared to be smashed economically by the power of the industrialized nations or whether we have the gumption to work with all the underdeveloped countries to protect our interests. No matter what they tell you in Washington about proper economic development, the fact of life is that the prices of what we produce are lower and lower on the world markets while the cost of manufactured goods and equipment we must buy from the industrialized countries keeps going up. The truth is that an economic abyss is being created and we shall be sucked into it unless we defend ourselves. So our allies are in Mexico and in Kenya and Ghana and in the Philippines and in Pakistan. This is not an ideological position: it's a pragmatic position, and you Americans know enough about pragmatics to understand that."

Some of Latin America's new alliances also have historical and cultural roots. With the emergence of independent African nations, Brazilians, Cubans and Haitians have begun to take pride in a heritage brought to the Americas by African slaves two and three centuries ago.

Brazil feels that because of her part-African background she can play an important role between Africa and the West. She has established embassies in African countries and has offered scholarships to African students.

Cuba's approach is different. Castro has the idea that his revolutionary notions have a place in Africa too, and Havana's relations with that continent are becoming increasingly important, especially in the case of the so-called radical states such as Algeria, the United Arab Republic, Ghana, Guinea, Tanzania and Mali. There are Cuban embassies in all the "radical" capitals, and hundreds of Africans are trained in Cuba in skills ranging from rice growing to guerrilla fighting. There is evidence that the 1964 revolution in Zanzibar (now part of Tanzania) was conducted by rebels trained in Cuba, and Castro is openly encouraging other revolts in Africa. Major Ernesto Che Guevara, Cuba's chief guerrilla expert, spent six weeks touring Africa early in 1965, and copies of his classic manual, *War of the Guerrillas*, are available in English, French and reportedly Swahili the length and breadth of the continent.

Haiti, Latin America's only Negro republic, has been playing up her African heritage since President François Duvalier came to power in 1957. Duvalier, a physician known to his followers as "Papa Doc," has steadily encouraged a sense of Africanism among Haitians as part of his violent dictatorial rule, which emphasizes absolute obedience along with the practice of voodoo.

It is sad that many Haitian schoolteachers fled the country to teach in the new African lands after Duvalier terrorized the intellectuals and middle class. Without teachers and technicians, Haiti is foundering in misery and corruption. In place of the economic and social development going on elsewhere in Latin America, there is brutal repression. This can be dangerous to an outsider too, as I found out on my last visit to Haiti some years ago.

It was a time when conspiracies against Duvalier, strongly encouraged from Washington, seemed to be developing and a task force of United States Marines waited offshore to land if serious violence flared. One night several bombs exploded in Port-au-Prince, the capital, and Duvalier's militia, the "Tonton-Macoutes" (literally "Bogeymen"), were out in strength.

I was in a taxi with another *Times* reporter and two more newsmen when screaming Tontons forced our cab to a halt in a dark street, dragged us out bodily at gunpoint and searched us for weapons. I had been caught up in mob violence many times in Latin America, but never before had I been so frightened. As we awaited the arrival of a Tonton chief we were guarded by men and boys armed with pistols and clubs. One youth stood behind me with two big rocks in his hands as if ready for an order to crack my head between them.

The Tontons were chattering in Creole, the Haitian dialect, and I understood enough of it to catch remarks like "Let's kill the white men" and "Papa Doc will be pleased if we do away with his enemies." The situation can be appreciated, I think, by some of my colleagues who covered the Congo or by a fellow *Times* correspondent who was caught by a hostile mob in Panama some years ago and had a rope placed around his neck, presumably in preparation for a summary hanging. But, as in the case of the *Times* man in Panama, we were saved by the arrival of the chief, who laughed off the whole affair and let us go. He turned out, incidentally, to be a professional tourist guide doubling as a Tonton boss.

Latin America and Africa are linked by other

factors besides economic underdevelopment and some cultural ties. In both parts of the world there are still colonies and the "colonialists" are resented.

While Britain granted independence to Jamaica and Trinidad in the early nineteen-sixties, British Guiana remains a colony because the bitter feud between its East Indians and Negroes has so far made a grant of independence inadvisable. British Guiana, with a population of less than 600,000, is an intriguing microcosm of a colonial problem. While East Indians and Negroes are in the majority, there are also Chinese, Portuguese and so-called Amerindian groups. Sugar, the main source of wealth, is owned by a British corporation. The field workers are East Indians. Civil servants and a large proportion of the inhabitants of Georgetown, the capital, are Negroes. The East Indians, who came as indentured workers from the Bombay and Madras areas in the last century, also control the trade. The colony is a patchwork of races and conflicting interests that have exploded into murderous violence. British Guiana's former Premier, Dr. Cheddi B. Jagan, a dentist of East Indian descent, went to live in Cuba after he was virtually forced out of office in an election in which all the other political groups united against his left-wing People's Progressive party. It was necessary to amend the electoral law to insure Jagan's defeat, but the British think it averted a revolution and terrible bloodshed.

In Central America, London would like to grant British Honduras independence soon, but the colony is claimed by Guatemala. The Guatemalans have threatened to take it over if the British ever pull out.

The British-Argentine dispute over the bleak islands in the South Atlantic that the British call the Falklands and the Argentines call the Malvinas has been going on for close to a century and a half and there is no sign that London will give them up or that Buenos Aires will forget about them. They remain a constant irritant. There are also, of course, French and Dutch possessions in Latin America and not all their inhabitants are happy about their lot.

On everything from colonial questions to commodity prices, Latin America has taken significant steps to assert herself on the international scene, leaving behind the pattern of isolation that Paraguay's dictator Francia symbolized more than a hundred years ago. Latin-American economists hold the floor in Geneva, Brazilian airliners fly to Tokyo and Beirut, Cuban revolutionaries preach violence in Africa, and at the U.N. other Latin Americans work to keep the whole world from exploding. It is all a far cry from the days of El Supremo.

III

The Role of the United States

BECAUSE OF GEOGRAPHY, economics and political and strategic considerations, the United States plays an overwhelmingly powerful role in the life of Latin America. Not surprisingly, then, the United States looms to many Latin Americans as the "Colossus of the North," and inevitably the immensely weighty U.S. presence has aroused anti-Yankeeism.

Over the years there have been anti-American demonstrations for every imaginable reason in every Latin-American capital. Embassies, consulates and libraries have been stoned, the Star-Spangled Banner has been burned and so, in effigy, have Uncle Sam and Presidents Eisenhower, Kennedy and Johnson. Former Vice President Nixon was the object of mob rage in Lima, Peru, and Caracas, Venezuela, during his famous "goodwill tour" in 1958. American property has been seized, confiscated or nationalized in several countries, and Americans have been molested and maligned.

These are external manifestations of the turbulence through which Latin America has been going for years. Her frustration at being an underdeveloped region often turns against the United States in a rebellion against authority, against political and economic size and power, and almost against a history that let North America grow in wealth but held Latin America back in poverty,

In a real sense, however, Latin America's relationship with the United States is much more subtle and complex. It includes what a psychologist would call a "love-hate relationship," a blending of resentment and admiration.

Latin America started out, of course, by loving North America. The American Revolution and the United States Constitution inspired the Latin-American revolutions for independence and the Latin-American constitutions. In the Spanish-American War, fought in 1898, the Yankees had Latin America's sympathies.

Then, halfway through this historical process, some hate seeped into the relationship. President Theodore Roosevelt's detaching of the province of Panama from Colombia so that he could build the Panama Canal rankled many in Latin America. The

Platt Amendment to Cuba's Constitution, forced
upon the newly freed island to give the U.S. the right
of intervention, was the original seed of Castro's
anti-American revolution nearly 60 years later. I remember Castro's speaking of the Platt Amendment
as if it were a present-day reality, even though President Franklin D. Roosevelt had abrogated it as far
back as 1934.

People have long memories and politicians have
often found it useful to play on those memories. The
Mexicans, for example, still think of the Veracruz
attack of 1914 as an event of last week, even though
the general relationship between the U.S. and Mexico is now remarkably harmonious. Americans may
think that President Woodrow Wilson was acting
correctly when he moved against Victoriano Huerta
just before World War I to restore democracy in
Mexico, but to Mexicans this was intervention by
the northern "colossus" and to this day Mexican
foreign policy is based on the concept of nonintervention.

To most Americans the name Smedley Butler
means nothing. But in the Caribbean it belongs to
the local demonology. Smedley Butler was the brigadier general who led the first occupation of the Dominican Republic by U.S. Marines in 1916 and was
credited with the famous remark that he was going
to make that country "safe for the boys of the National City Bank."

Shortly after Generalissimo Rafael Leonidas Trujillo Molina, the Dominican dictator, was assassinated in 1961, the ghost of Smedley Butler—perhaps prophetically—came to the fore. I was visiting a leading politician of the Fourteenth of June Movement, a Castro-like revolutionary group, and as soon as the conversation touched on U.S.-Dominican relations General Butler was brought back to life.

"We cannot forget Smedley Butler that easily," the Dominican declared.

"I beg your pardon?" I said.

"Yes," he went on, "the memory of General Butler lives among us. It was Butler who brought the Marines here, then his successors created Trujillo and for 31 years you Americans tolerated and abetted the dictatorship."

To be sure, most Dominicans are not so concerned as this politician was about Smedley Butler; probably few even know much about him. But the record does show that it was the United States that sponsored Trujillo in the Marine-trained constabulary and then looked the other way when he took power. The memory of this, of course, returned in full force after United States troops again had to land in the Dominican Republic in 1965.

On the other hand, the United States was aware of the 1961 conspiracy to kill Trujillo and sympathetic to the idea of removing him from power. This

I brought up in my conversation with the leftist who had been damning Smedley Butler.

"Well," he replied, "I don't think you can wash blood away with blood. Or call it poetic justice or overdue retribution. I, for one, would argue that the Americans simply concluded that Trujillo had lost his usefulness and that it was time to create a new and more convenient stooge."

This conversation is a good example of an attitude that prevails among some—but by no means the majority—of Latin Americans. The basic argument, usually put forth by ultranationalistic and leftist groups, is that *everything* the United States does in Latin America stems from a sinister design to maintain control over the region. Thus the United States was to be blamed for *not* aiding Latin America—the better to keep her subservient, the critics cried. But when the Alliance for Progress was launched to aid Latin America, the same critics charged that this Kennedy program was a plot to perpetuate domination by U.S. economic interests.

I have heard this argument in innumerable discussions with students, intellectuals and leftist politicians and reached the grudging conclusion that in the view of some Latin Americans the United States is damned if it does and damned if it doesn't.

This "Smedley Butler syndrome," as an American ambassador of my acquaintance once called it, persists in all the countries where there have been

American armed interventions earlier in this century. Aside from the Dominican Republic and Mexico, it is found in Panama, Haiti and Nicaragua. In Nicaragua the U.S.—and its Marines—are blamed for creating the dictatorship of the late Anastasio Somoza (the man who kept a black panther in a cage at his palace) in a manner similar to the American-sponsored rise of Trujillo.

In Panama the historical resentment against the United States stretches back to 1903, when Teddy Roosevelt sponsored a revolution that led to the detachment of the isthmus from Colombia so that the Panama Canal could be built on American terms. Ever since, Panama's entire sovereign life has been colored by problems with the United States over this waterway.

The Canal was—and largely is—Panama's main economic resource. Much more important than the direct profits from Canal tolls, the waterway has provided employment and created important investments in the country. Because of the Canal the merchant class has prospered.

Yet this prosperity has not seeped down to the mass of the Panamanian people. The oligarchy—those who earned fortunes from the American presence, imitated Americans and still profoundly resented them—never allowed other Panamanians to share the wealth. Until recently, moreover, discrimination in employment against Panamanian workers

barred them from many benefits. Job and other fa-
voritism was enjoyed by the Americans dwelling in
the narrow Canal Zone, a strip of land across Panama granted in perpetuity to the United States in
1903 under Teddy Roosevelt's treaty.

Long-simmering bitterness finally erupted in the
bloody riots of January, 1964, in which both Panamanians and Americans were killed. Diplomatic relations between Panama and the United States were
broken and three months elapsed before mediators
from the Organization of American States finally
succeeded in working out a settlement.

The crux of Panama's demands was the abroga-
tion of the 1903 treaty's provisions under which the
United States enjoys virtually sovereign status in the
Canal Zone. The Johnson Administration refused to
commit itself to this, though it agreed to enter into
full-fledged discussions with Panama on all subjects.
Then, in December, 1964, President Johnson announced that the United States planned to build a
new canal, a sea-level waterway, across Panama or
neighboring lands to accommodate growing traffic.
He indicated that the United States would renegoti-
ate the 1903 treaty covering the old Canal's status
while negotiations were under way with Panama
and three other countries for the projected new
waterway.

All U.S. problems in Latin America did not stem
from old interventions. Inevitably the magnitude of

the American economic presence was another source of friction. In many instances United States corporations gained overwhelming political influence in the countries in which they operated. Such a state of affairs existed after the turn of the century and well into the years following World War II in many of the Caribbean and Central American republics, where United States investors owned vast fruit and sugar plantations and extensive cattle land. U.S. investors also exercised considerable influence in petroleum-producing Venezuela and in the mining nations of Chile and Peru.

To an overwhelming extent this influence has come to an end. The role of U.S. capital has changed almost everywhere in keeping with new political realities and the enlightenment of the American entrepreneur. In many countries foreign capital is subject to stringent regulations and is actively cooperating with national economic development plans.

In Venezuela the onetime oil-company towns have been replaced by new cities with rising living standards. One of the largest American corporations in that country has established a multimillion-dollar foundation to encourage Venezuelan cultural and intellectual life. In Peru an American oil company has erected a model workers' city. Elsewhere the trend has been for American investors to sell their interests in public utilities, a politically sensitive area of the economy, and reinvest in general manufacturing.

Today, with more than $8 billion invested in Latin America, U.S. private capital is a major positive factor in economic development. However, old resentments are not altogether forgotten and leftists and ultranationalists not surprisingly strive to keep them alive for political purposes.

In the area of United States Government cooperation with Latin America, notable advances have been made through the Alliance for Progress. This program has served to increase and coordinate earlier U.S. lending efforts, many of which fell short of taking into account the over-all requirements of each country.

Under the Alliance, United States commitments to Latin America have ranged from $1 billion to $1.5 billion annually since 1961. These funds have gone into "institution building"—the creation of housing, land-reform and economic-planning institutions—as well as into actual development projects ranging from farm resettlement to new housing and industries.

The concept of the Alliance as set forth in its Charter, formulated at a 1961 conference in Punta del Este, Uruguay, calls not only for United States funds but also for Latin-American self-help and international private investment. The Inter-American Development Bank, in which the U.S. is a major partner, is another major source of capital. Lately efforts have been made to encourage investment by Western European countries.

Besides the Alliance for Progress, which provides money and technical expertise, the U.S. has made another major contribution to Latin America's development. This is the Peace Corps. By all accounts, it has been one of the most successful U.S. efforts in Latin America as elsewhere in the world, teaching individuals everything from community development to library planning and chicken farming. Since a developing society can succeed only if its grass-roots members acquire the skills they need to take advantage of broad economic and social advancement plans, the Peace Corps volunteers have played a vital role in much of Latin America.

In addition, the presence of these young men and women has done extraordinarily much to improve the public image of the United States. The enthusiastic and dedicated volunteers, living in villages and urban slums, have become identified with the local populations and their needs and aspirations. In terms of goodwill the Peace Corps is probably the most effective single United States effort in the Western Hemisphere.

Yet even the Alliance for Progress and the Peace Corps cannot overnight construct an era of universal good feeling between the United States and Latin America. The real and imagined grievances are still there on both sides. The rough edges of the Latin-American revolution cause frequent anger among United States citizens. And what the Latin Americans regard as the slowness of the *Norte Americanos* to comprehend their problems—or simply to give in to all their demands—is a constant source of friction. Such events as the Dominican intervention in the spring of 1965 tend to revive old fears that the "Colossus of the North" is on another rampage.

Obviously, much time and greater stability in Latin America will be required to set the relationship with the United States on an even keel. Meanwhile the old love-hate relationship will persist, sometimes vividly and dramatically, sometimes imperceptibly, for this is the way of history.

IV

The Dominican Crisis

IN THE EARLY EVENING of Wednesday, April 28, 1965, a flight of khaki-painted helicopters took off from the deck of the U.S.S. *Boxer* and whirred some 10 miles over the Caribbean to the coast of the Dominican Republic.

In twos and threes they landed on the Polo Grounds, immediately west of the Hotel Embajador in Santo Domingo, as dusk began to gather over the capital city. Combat-equipped Marines, jumping out of the choppers as soon as they touched down, could hear explosions and machine-gun fire in the downtown section, a few miles to the east. These were the sounds of the raging civil war in which Dominicans were dying by the hundreds; the established order had utterly collapsed in revolutionary chaos. And as the tough Marines from the Navy's Amphibious Task Force began streaming ashore, the first United States military intervention in the Dominican Republic in nearly 49 years was under way.

In less than a week the initial contingent of 520 Marines, who had landed in Santo Domingo to protect the evacuation of Americans and other foreigners from the war-battered city, had grown to an imposing force of 22,000 men, including a whole Marine brigade and the Army's entire 82nd Airborne Division. Eight thousand additional men aboard 40 warships cruising offshore and an around-the-clock airlift of troop carriers from the United States supported the American expeditionary force in Santo Domingo.

As the month of May began, the United States forces that had at first landed on a humanitarian mission found themselves under orders from Washington to restore peace between the warring factions and, in the words of an official announcement, to "help Dominicans find a democratic solution" to their awesome political problems.

The American intervention in the Dominican Republic was the first instance since 1934—the year the Marines were withdrawn from Haiti—of United States forces, in effect, occupying a Latin-American country or part of one. It was a move that had not been chanced even in the case of Cuba, a Communist-dominated nation honeycombed with Soviet weapons and advisers. It was a move that seemed to flout all of the United States commitments to avoid unilateral intervention. It was a move that appeared to defy all the inter-American treaties signed since the United States renounced its rights of intervention 31 years earlier.

Why, then, had President Johnson ordered the Dominican intervention of 1965, which was from the outset deeply controversial and which has had a considerable effect on the entire fabric of United States relations with Latin America?

To try to understand the situation that brought about this intervention as well as the factors that may have motivated President Johnson, it is necessary to look at the recent political history of the Dominican Republic.

That history begins with the ouster of Juan Bosch in a military coup d'état on September 25, 1963, after he had served for seven months as the country's first constitutional president in 38 years.

Bosch, a gifted writer and self-taught political scientist, won the 1962 elections with 62 per cent of the votes in what loomed as the beginning of a new, promising and democratic future for the Dominican Republic. I covered these elections for *The Times* and vividly remember the immense pride that Dominicans felt in voting freely for the first time in a generation. A red ink mark on the index finger, signifying that a person had voted, was displayed as a badge of distinction.

Lyndon Johnson, then Vice President of the United States, and Hubert H. Humphrey, then Majority Whip in the Senate, led the U.S. delegation to Dr. Bosch's inauguration on February 27, 1963. It was a moment of warm feelings between Americans and Dominicans, for the Dominicans remembered that only 16 months earlier the United States had been ready to land Marines to remove the heirs of the Trujillo dictatorship and protect the nascent democratic process. There are photographs of Mr. Johnson and Dr. Bosch in smiling embrace.

With the Kennedy Administration determined to make the post-Trujillo Dominican Republic the "showcase of democracy" in the Caribbean as a contrast to neighboring Cuba, the Bosch government appeared to be off to a promising start. Alliance for Progress funds were being channeled into the country, American technicians were arriving to help in its development, and ambitious plans were being drawn up for power and irrigation dams to benefit the quickly growing population of nearly four million.

But as Dr. Bosch himself had written a few years before he returned from a quarter-century of exile to run for President, the Dominican Republic was "cursed" by the fates from the day Christopher Columbus set foot there in 1492. Things began going wrong as soon as the triumphant *vivas* of Bosch's inauguration died down in the ancient city of Santo Domingo by the blue Caribbean.

The losers in the 1962 elections wasted no time in talking about a coup if "Bosch gets out of hand." Those in the business community and among the wealthy landowners who had opposed Bosch became the nucleus of agitation against him. This is not to say, incidentally, that all or even the majority of businessmen and landowners were anti-Bosch; an important segment of these groups had supported him. This is why it is inaccurate to state, as many have, that the entire Dominican "oligarchy" opposed Bosch and his notions of gradual social reform.

However, the anti-Bosch civilian groups quickly found allies among military officers, particularly the older ones, who had served in Trujillo's armed forces. One of the important things to keep in mind about the Dominican situation is that, despite Trujillo's assassination and the shift to a democratic experiment after 1961, the old dictator's armed forces were never touched—that is, most of the former commanders remained where they were. This is a major reason why the tradition of brutality, dictatorship and corruption did not die with Trujillo.

The right-wing civilians and the Trujillo military came together to form the battering ram that smashed Dominican democracy through the anti-

Bosch coup. The immediate charges voiced against Bosch were that he harbored or protected Communists and that corruption was spreading in the country. The latter was a surprising charge, considering the source.

As to the Communism charge, it never went beyond vague accusations that Bosch allowed pro-Castro Dominicans to travel to and from Cuba and that Communist parties were tolerated in the Dominican Republic. Bosch's retort was that after three decades of tyranny it would be a poor idea to start proscribing *any* political parties, even the Communists. He pointed out that Communist parties were legal in the United States and most of Western Europe as well as in several Latin-American countries. But his main argument was that the limited Communist and pro-Castro influences in the Dominican Republic could better be fought with the implementation of a functioning democracy and with economic and social development than with police methods.

Yet the charges, played up in some United States newspapers and loudly repeated by Bosch's enemies at home, did their damage. The fact that the Bosch administration was far from efficient and that the new President embroiled himself in problems with the military added to the pressures against him.

Finally, on September 25, 1963, the military moved and Bosch was ousted and again exiled. The new rulers at first spoke of a "rightist state," then dropped the idea when it became apparent that, contrary to what they had heard from their friends among American military officers, the Kennedy Administration was determined to punish the coup. In fact, diplomatic relations were broken, Alliance for Progress aid was suspended and U.S. technicians were pulled out.

The next step was the creation of a three-man civilian junta—the "Triumvirate"—operating with military support and making vague promises of restoring democracy. Wtih Bosch's own Dominican Revolutionary party offering no opposition to the coup, the only action against the new regime came from the pro-Castro Fourteenth of June Movement, headed by Manuel Tavares Justo. Tavares and a handful of his followers took to the hills in what they hoped would be a repetition of Castro's successful guerrilla movement. But nobody in the country was interested in supporting them—which gave force to Bosch's argument about the weakness of Dominican Communism and Castroism—and in mid-December, 1963, army troops flushed out and killed the guerrillas.

Sentiment in the Dominican Republic against the killing of the guerrillas after they had surrendered was so strong that Triumvirate President Emilio de los Santos resigned in protest. However, the Johnson Administration concluded that the new regime needed some form of support, and diplomatic relations were presently re-established.

For the next year or so the Dominican Republic lived in a state of comparative calm. The 'Triumvirate had, for all practical purposes, disappeared. The administration was in the hands of Donald Reid Cabral, a former auto dealer who had been active first in the anti-Trujillo conspiracy and then in the Council of State Government that supervised the elections which gave Bosch his short-lived victory.

Reid Cabral, who aided Bosch's overthrow, apparently worked hard to lead the Dominican Republic to some form of economic recovery. He followed closely the advice of the United States and of international financial institutions. His rule was rather authoritarian but not dictatorial, and after a while he became increasingly involved in struggles with the old military establishment. To curb their privileges and influence, Reid Cabral successively dismissed a number of the top commanders, finally taking over the Ministry of Defense himself.

But Reid Cabral somehow could never win popularity or establish any rapport with other political forces, and the country grew more and more restive. He announced elections for September, 1965, making it clear not only that he would run for the presidency but that, most likely, he would win.

It was this matter of the elections that sealed his fate and set in motion the preparations for a new revolution. The revolutionary movement was led by a group of younger military officers who had resented Bosch's overthrow and by key members of Bosch's political party. The revolt was actually planned for June 1, 1965, but Reid Cabral became aware of the conspiracy and in mid-April fired seven air-force officers who were among the plotters.

This precipitated the explosion. On the afternoon of Saturday, April 24, a group of civilians captured Radio Santo Domingo, the government's radio and television station, and broadcast announcements that the regime had fallen. Simultaneously the military rebels took control of two army barracks, one in Santo Domingo and one on the outskirts.

Crowds poured out into the streets to celebrate the revolution's apparent victory with shouts of "Bosch!" and "Constitution!" But government forces promptly retook the radio station, and during the evening Reid Cabral announced that the rebellion had been smashed. The government then issued an ultimatum to the rebels holding the two military installations to surrender by 6:00 A.M. of the next day or face attacks by war planes and tanks.

The United States Embassy in Santo Domingo, which had been surprised when the revolt erupted on Saturday, advised the State Department in Washington that matters were well in hand. Ambassador W. Tapley Bennett, Jr., and the head of the economic aid mission and 11 of the 13 members of the

United States Military Advisory Assistance Mission were away from the Dominican Republic at the time of the revolution. But the officials at the embassy, most of whose contacts were with the Reid Cabral regime, were convinced that the Saturday rebellion was a minor matter.

How wrong they were, however, became apparent during the night. Shortly before midnight crowds again began pouring into the downtown streets, this time not to celebrate but to clamor for a return to "constitutionality"—the battle cry of the revolutionaries. A telephone campaign was started by students, urging people to come out and demonstrate. Someone went into a firehouse and turned on the siren, adding to the tension.

Meanwhile military commanders of different factions were in contact and tacitly reached the decision that, no matter what else happened, Reid Cabral had to go. The old-line commanders resented him because he had curtailed their power; the younger officers wanted him removed because of their demands for a restoration of legal rule. For a few hours all the military were in agreement that the Reid Cabral regime must be ousted—this was the only time there had been agreement on anything among them.

At dawn of Sunday, April 25, the commanders converged on the Presidential Palace and forced Reid Cabral to resign. He did so promptly, convinced that his ultimatum to the rebels would not be obeyed. Reid Cabral resigned on the understanding that a military junta would be formed to rule the country until elections could be held in some distant future. And this, too, was the understanding of the commanders from the San Isidro Air Force Base across the Ozama River from Santo Domingo, where the bulk of the elite forces were stationed.

But the young officers who had precipitated the revolt the day before had other ideas. Moving swiftly, they proclaimed that the revolution for the return of Bosch had triumphed. Instantly they swore in a Provisional President until Bosch could arrive from exile in Puerto Rico. The Provisional President was José Rafael Molina Ureña, who had been President of the Chamber of Deputies during the Bosch government. He was constitutionally in line for the succession in the absence of the President, the Vice President and the head of the Senate. Colonel Miguel Angel Hernando Ramírez, one of the chiefs of the military rebel movement, became Secretary of Defense.

The pro-Bosch move that Sunday morning was the act that set off what was to be a bloody civil war. The commanders at the San Isidro base, notably Brigadier General Elias Wessin y Wessin, who had led the Bosch ouster coup in 1963, could not accept a restoration of constitutional rule. The lines were drawn. In the afternoon Wessin's aircraft strafed the

Presidential Palace in the opening action of the fratricidal conflict.

That same afternoon I met with Juan Bosch, having arrived in Puerto Rico from Washington a few hours earlier en route to Santo Domingo. The Bosch home, a modest second-floor apartment in a residential section of San Juan, was all joy and confusion. Friends and former aides of Dr. Bosch were there in force. Mrs. Bosch and other members of the family were packing for what they expected to be their immediate return to Santo Domingo. They hoped a Dominican military aircraft would fly to San Juan to take them back after 19 months of exile. Only Bosch, an immensely self-controlled man, was calm. He made a remark to me that in the light of later events turned out to be very significant. "Nobody from the United States Government has contacted me thus far," he said. "Why?"

One part of the answer to his question was in the U.S. Embassy in Santo Domingo and the other part in Washington. At the embassy the feeling was that the Bosch movement still had no chance of success. Much of this feeling stemmed, of course, from the embassy's close identification with the Reid Cabral regime and with many of the military commanders who had overthrown Bosch. At the State Department in Washington the judgment was that Bosch's return could mean "Communism in Santo Domingo within six months," though nobody could document this assertion for the record. However, the genesis of what the United States was to do in the Dominican Republic in the next few days was to be found in these initial attitudes and judgments in Santo Domingo and Washington.

In Santo Domingo, meanwhile, matters were not going well for the rebels. Although the provisional government controlled the city, the Wessin forces held the San Isidro base and the approaches to the Ozama River bridge that led into the capital. All day Monday Wessin's P-51 fighters and Gloster Meteor jets strafed and bombed the city and the strategic bridge. The rebels in the streets countered by employing mirrors that reflected the sun's rays in an attempt to momentarily blind the pilots of the diving aircraft. Families of the pilots were detained and brought before television cameras to make appeals to the fliers to desist from the attacks. Others were taken to the bridge as hostages.

As early as Sunday the rebel command had realized that to counter the offensive of the San Isidro forces it must start arming civilians. At first it announced that military veterans could receive arms if they signed a receipt. But within hours it was decided to throw open the doors of city arsenals and army barracks to one and all. Several truckloads of weapons were brought in from the suburban barracks and placed at the downtown Parque Independencia for all to help themselves.

This was a major factor in aggravating the civil war and in influencing the subsequent U.S. decision to intervene. Weapons were now not only in the hands of the pro-Bosch civilians but also in the hands of Communists, Castroites and plain adventurers and thrill-seekers. Bands of *tigres*—hoodlums—were organized along with the fairly disciplined groups of military and civilian rebels.

In an effort to capture the capital, General Wessin brought up tanks, artillery and infantry of the air force (the air force is virtually a separate army in the Dominican Republic) and of his own tough and highly indoctrinated Armed Forces Training Center. Full-fledged warfare raged in the old city for control of the bridge as the rebels countered with their tanks and artillery. Elsewhere armed bands roamed Santo Domingo. Men fired from roofs and windows, sometimes aimlessly, and others responded from street corners and hideouts. Casualties—mainly civilians—were mounting.

Late on Monday the Wessin forces captured the bridge and began entering the city but were repulsed. That same evening the United States decided that a "voluntary" evacuation of Americans should be undertaken because of the growing danger to them from the armed bands. There had, however, been no incident thus far involving Americans.

Embassy officials reported to Washington that it appeared that pro-Communist elements were taking control of the rebellion—mainly because Castro-like broadcasts were being made on radio and television as soldiers and young officers denounced their superiors. Up to then, however, the embassy had had no contact with the rebels except for a visit to the embassy on Sunday afternoon by a group of leaders of the Bosch party, including a former Minister of Agriculture named Silvestre Antonio Guzmán, who was to become highly important in subsequent developments. According to Mr. Guzmán, the delegation was "virtually insulted" by a second secretary of the embassy.

Early Tuesday, April 27, as the ships of the Navy's Amphibious Task Force began moving into position for the evacuation operation, other U.S. forces were being alerted. Several battalions of Marines at Camp Lejeune, North Carolina, were placed on alert. The tough 82nd Airborne Division at Fort Bragg, North Carolina, was told to prepare for a "parachute attack" on the Dominican Republic. Its orders were to secure the San Isidro Air Force Base, the highway leading to the Ozama River bridge and the bridge itself. This indicated that as early as Tuesday morning the Johnson Administration was already thinking in terms of a major military operation.

On Tuesday morning evacuation ships entered the port of Haina, nine miles west of Santo Domingo. Helicopters flew to the Polo Grounds by the

Hotel Embajador, in the western section of the city, to help in the evacuation. American and other foreign families began gathering at the hotel early in the morning to be processed by embassy officials and driven to Haina. A few armed Marines, acting as helicopter guards, were at the Polo Grounds.

In mid-morning a band of armed civilians broke into the hotel, apparently searching for a television commentator identified with General Wessin. They forced the Americans to line up against the walls of the cavernous lobby and fired several submachine-gun bursts over their heads. This experience, later exaggerated in the reports to Washington, was another major factor in influencing President Johnson to order a full-scale intervention.

In downtown Santo Domingo, meanwhile, the fighting at the bridge raged all day. General Wessin's aircraft hit the bridge area and the Presidential Palace. The frigates and destroyers of the small Dominican Navy, which at first seemed to be supporting the rebels, took up positions facing the city. In the early afternoon they lobbed three shells into the sector of the Presidential Palace.

Then a new act in the mounting drama opened at the United States Embassy. Ambassador Bennett, who was flown in from Washington and reached the embassy at noon Tuesday, received in mid-afternoon a visit from eight or nine rebel officers, including Colonel Hernando Ramírez. They told him that there had been "enough bloodshed," that the rebellion was seemingly failing and that they hoped he would mediate between rebels and Wessin forces.

The Ambassador replied, that, while he was not authorized to mediate, he could contact the Wessin command to see what terms might be granted the rebels. Then a request was made to Mr. Bennett to seek to persuade Provisional President Molina Ureña to resign so that the rebellion could be ended.

An embassy official was dispatched to the Presidential Palace, a few blocks away. He found Molina Ureña sitting dejectedly in the only occupied room in the building. The rest of the palace was empty. Windows were smashed and there was rubble here and there from the direct hits in the air attacks.

According to an embassy account, Molina Ureña was at first reluctant to give up the fight. His associates, however, prevailed upon him. An hour later the Provisional President and some 18 rebel officers arrived at the embassy. Again they asked Mr. Bennett to mediate and again he told them that he could only communicate with the San Isidro base on the terms the rebels could expect. The meeting broke up on a note of defeat on the part of the rebels, and Molina Ureña drove directly to the Colombian Embassy to request asylum. The U.S. Embassy assumed that the rebellion had collapsed, and apparently only a few officials paid much attention to a parting remark by a rebel officer, Colonel Francisco Caamaño Denó, that "we shall go on fighting."

Fight they did. During the night Colonel Caamaño reorganized his forces and entrenched himself in the rectangular area of downtown Santo Domingo. Now the rebels seemed more defiant than ever. The next morning—Wednesday, April 28—a military junta was sworn in at San Isidro. It was headed by Colonel Pedro Benoit, a virtually unknown air-force officer, and there are reasons to believe the U.S. Embassy favored it. At least the junta was a body for the United States to deal with.

Fighting continued throughout the day, and in the early afternoon Colonel Benoit telephoned Ambassador Bennett to say that his forces could not assure the protection of foreigners in Santo Domingo and that he requested a "temporary intervention." A few hours later Colonel Benoit sent the Ambassador a note confirming his request for intervention.

Now the stage was set for the first U.S. landing. Ambassador Bennett relayed the Benoit intervention request to the State Department and the White House shortly before 6:00 P.M., Washington time. He added his own recommendation for a landing. There was scattered firing around the embassy as Mr. Bennett telephoned to the White House.

At the White House President Johnson told his aides that he had to act on the intervention request, and Secretary of Defense Robert S. McNamara relayed the order to General Earle G. Wheeler, Chair-

man of the Joint Chiefs of Staff. Immediately the
flash went out to the Navy.

I was standing on the flying bridge of U.S.S.
Wood County, a Navy LST of the Amphibious Task
Force, when the Presidential flash—"PREPARE TO
LAND"—was relayed by the ship's radio system at
7:10 P.M., Caribbean time. Within minutes helicopters began taking off from the U.S.S. *Boxer,* the helicopter carrier that was the flagship of the task force,
ferrying Marines to the Polo Grounds. The intervention had begun.

I was among the newsmen who were being taken
to the Dominican Republic by the Navy, virtually
the only way of entering the country at war. During
the night ammunition was issued to the Marines
aboard, and preparations were made to land the artillery and armored personnel carriers.

The next morning we came into sight of the
Boxer. Helicopters were shuttling back and forth between the warship and the Hotel Embajador, bringing evacuees to the *Boxer,* and flying Marines
ashore. Jeeps and other equipment were transported
by other choppers. Santo Domingo could be seen
through the morning haze. Shortly before noon we
were transferred by highline to the *Boxer.* After a
quick cup of Navy coffee we were loaded aboard
Marine helicopters for the hop to the Polo Grounds.

The Hotel Embajador, now the temporary opera-
tional center for United States forces, was filled with

refugees awaiting evacuation. There was almost no food at the hotel and no power or water. Marines were digging in around the perimeter of the hotel.

In mid-afternoon the embassy again came under sniper fire. A platoon of Marines, who had moved there during the previous night, fought off the attackers, but at least one Marine was hit.

Santo Domingo, meanwhile, was a battlefield. After regrouping, the rebels had regained the initiative and now were pressing for control of the Ozama River bridge, hoping to break out into the San Isidro area. They were besieging the Ozama Fortress in the old city, where hundreds of riot policemen loyal to the junta were defending a vast arsenal of weapons.

The first newsmen to venture into the downtown section found it a hell. The hospitals were unable to tend to the hundreds of casualties. They were running out of medical supplies. They had no water or electricity. Wounded men and women were often operated upon while lying on the floor. Most were left to die because nothing could be done for them. The bodies were then dumped out into the yards and burned to prevent an epidemic.

Working in these tragic conditions in the Santo Domingo hospitals were six Peace Corps nurses, perhaps the greatest unsung heroines of the civil war. Despite continuous firing and air attacks, these girls remained at their posts for two weeks until finally ordered out of the hospitals by their American supervisors. They returned later and drove ambulances carrying the wounded from the rebel area to United States Army field hospitals. I talked to them on many occasions. They were unpretentious, unimpressed by the hardships and danger they had undergone, casual and good-humored. They had worked with Dominicans for more than a year in community development projects in the capital's slums and housing projects, and they felt that it was simply their duty to remain with the people who had become their friends. In an article I remarked that the Peace Corps in Santo Domingo was the real "great American story." I still think so, looking back at those awesome days.

Late Thursday night—April 29—the advance elements of the 82nd Airborne Division began landing at San Isidro, securing the air base and immediately moving out toward the Ozama River bridge. The U.S. intervention was now in high gear as additional Marine units landed at Haina and the Polo Grounds and as paratroopers poured into San Isidro.

The next morning—Friday—tank-led Marines fanned out of the Hotel Embajador's grounds to occupy a nine-square-mile area in the western residential section of Santo Domingo. This area was to become the International Security Zone under the provisions of a resolution adopted in Washington the previous evening by the Council of the Organi-

zation of American States acting as a ministerial-
level organ of consultation. The Security Zone was
intended to create a perimeter within which refugees could be safely evacuated and most of the foreign embassies could be protected. The United
States Embassy was only a block from the zone's
border and was subjected to continuous sniper fire.

The first Marine to die in Santo Domingo was
killed that Friday morning. He was among the
troops moving cautiously along Nicolás de Pensón
Street toward the U.S. Embassy behind tanks and
armored personnel carriers. He was shot through
the head by a sniper.

By this time the embassy was convinced that
Communists had completely taken over the rebel
movement. The decisions in Washington were in ac-
cord with its reports from Santo Domingo. As evidence of the alleged Communist take-over, the embassy cited propaganda sheets signed by the three
Communist movements calling for resistance to the
Wessin forces and "imperialism"; posters, also
signed by these groups, urging "Arms for the People"; and the alleged presence of known Communists in positions of command. At no time, however,
did the embassy spell out for newsmen what Communists occupied what posts.

Actually there was never any doubt that the
Communists and their allies fully supported the rebellion and actively participated in it. As a foreign

diplomat in Santo Domingo remarked, "all the Communists are rebels—but not all the rebels are Communists." When American newsmen went downtown into the rebel zone, crowds surrounded them to say that "We are not Communists: we want the Constitution." Businessmen, lawyers and doctors were among those trying to convince the reporters that their movement was not Communist.

During those days of the first week of the revolution no United States official had any extensive contact with the rebels, though extensive contacts were maintained with the military junta at San Isidro. After the meeting with Molina Ureña and his officers, Ambassador Bennett and most of his aides made up their minds that those rebels who chose to go on fighting must be Communist-dominated.

In reality, however, the rebel command was an extraordinary collection of people. Colonel Caamaño himself, a 32-year-old career officer, was the United States-educated son of a leading Trujillo general. Nobody ever accused him of being pro-Communist, but it was assumed, though no evidence was offered, that he was under the thumb of Communists. His closest associate, a civilian politician named Héctor Aristy, was a businessman with New York and Washington lobbying connections. The top military leader, Colonel Ramón Monte Araches, was considered an ultranationalist rightist. Another leading military figure was a Frenchman named André

Rivière, who had served in Indochina and was reported to have been ousted from the French Army for membership in the right-wing terroristic Secret Army Organization.

Both Aristy and Rivière exercised considerable influence on Colonel Caamaño in the first days of the rebellion, but no U.S. official could name visible Communists in positions of command, although a list of 58 Communists allegedly connected with the movement was widely circulated by U.S. sources.

The impact of the embassy's insistence that the Caamaño movement was Communist-dominated resulted in determination in Washington that "another Cuba" would not be allowed in the Caribbean. On the strength of this interpretation of Dominican events more U.S. troops kept pouring into Santo Domingo and the United States became increasingly identified with the junta.

Meanwhile political changes of importance occurred in both factions. Bosch announced in Puerto Rico that he was renouncing his rights to the presidency, and a rump session of the Dominican Congress in Santo Domingo chose Colonel Caamaño as constitutional president. Also in Santo Domingo the United States sponsored the creation of a regime that succeeded the Benoit junta and took the name of Government of National Reconstruction. It was headed by Antonio Imbert Barreras, one of the two survivors of the conspiracy to assassinate Trujillo.

Imbert was an honorary general and, as events were to prove later, a remarkably talented politician.

While the fighting continued an O.A.S. commission and the O.A.S. Secretary General, José A. Mora, undertook efforts in cooperation with the Papal Nuncio, Monsignor Emanuele Clarizio, to negotiate a truce. They met with apparent success when both sides signed cease-fire documents on May 5. But the truce was at best tenuous.

United States paratroopers opened a corridor—a line of communications, in military parlance—across rebel territory from the International Security Zone in the west to the Ozama River bridge and the San Isidro base in the east. This had the effect of cutting in two the rebels' sector and, in time, making them vulnerable to attack by the Imbert junta.

Predictably, the Imbert regime broke the truce a week later. Its aircraft attacked the rebels' broadcasting station in the downtown area. This attack, which also threatened the U.S. Embassy as machine-gun bullets rained in the streets around it, had political consequences. Ambassador Bennett, the foremost American advocate of the junta, took cover under his office desk when the air raid came, then protested to the O.A.S. that the Imbert forces had violated the truce. By then the Imbert group had become identified with the United States, though the Johnson Administration insisted Washington was maintaining "strict neutrality" in the conflict.

Though Mr. Bennett and the embassy in Santo Domingo kept insisting that the rebel movement had Communist characteristics, and continued to favor the junta, second thoughts developed in Washington. The Administration became aware that in backing the Imbert junta it was backing an unpopular group and that this was having adverse effects in Latin America. It was only by one vote that the United States succeeded in obtaining an O.A.S. resolution creating an inter-American armed force for the Dominican Republic.

Some of the most influential Latin-American governments, including those normally friendly to the U.S., had opposed both the United States intervention and the subsequent efforts to turn it into an inter-American enterprise. Mexico, Chile, Peru, Ecuador and Uruguay voted against it. Others, such as Costa Rica and Venezuela, went along with the utmost reluctance. In fact, the bulk of U.S. support came from the countries with military governments or military-backed governments.

It was at this juncture that the Administration decided to try a new approach to the crisis. Bosch was contacted in San Juan by Abe Fortas, a Washington lawyer and personal friend of President Johnson (and now a Supreme Court Justice), and asked to seek a compromise formula. Bosch agreed to cooperate and proposed that Silvestre Antonio Guzmán, his former Minister of Agriculture and a wealthy planter, be chosen constitutional president.

The Administration agreed to explore this possibility, and McGeorge Bundy, President Johnson's special assistant for national security, flew secretly to San Juan with Deputy Secretary of Defense Cyrus R. Vance. From there they went on to Santo Domingo. With the United States committed publicly to support a constitutional coalition government in the Dominican Republic, the first task was to get General Imbert to agree to resign.

But Imbert, who had been put up by the embassy as a temporary arrangement, suddenly refused to resign, insisting that he was the legal President of the Dominican Republic. As a U.S. newsman wrote, "the United States discovered that its puppet was pulling his own strings." A stalemate developed that Washington could not resolve as it tried to steer a course between conflicting pressures and advice.

After ten days of negotiations with Mr. Guzmán, the rebels and the junta, Bundy returned to Washington late in May, unable to break the deadlock.

This deadlock had become even more difficult to resolve because the United States had refused to enforce the cease-fire, letting the Imbert forces overrun the northern part of the city, above the corridor the U.S. paratroopers had opened. There had been hundreds of additional casualties in this second round of heavy fighting as junta tanks and troops fired into houses, killing women and children.

Now the rebels were confined to a small section of downtown Santo Domingo, with United States paratroopers and Brazilian infantrymen separating— and, in a sense, protecting—them from the junta forces. The initial United States judgment, after Washington allowed the Imbert command to take the north of the city, was that the military stalemate would lead to a political compromise.

But more than three months were to elapse before a settlement of sorts was reached—and even then it was not a compromise. Because of the junta's refusal to accept a provisional regime under Héctor García-Godoy, another former Bosch cabinet minister backed by the United States and the O.A.S., the Johnson Administration finally struck down its erstwhile protégé by depriving General Imbert of financial support. In the end, an agreement was signed on September 3—with Colonel Caamaño signing for the rebels and a junta officer for the opposing band—setting up the provisional regime.

How tenuous this settlement seemed to be, however, was proved immediately by a U.S. move to deport General Wessin y Wessin, another of its onetime protégés, and by the continuing tensions and incidents that were heightened by Dr. Bosch's belated return to his homeland late in September. With the whole Dominican outlook still highly uncertain, chances were that U.S. troops would have to remain for a long time in that hate-torn republic.

V

The Organization of
American States

THE DOMINICAN CRISIS was a great milestone for
the Organization of American States, which was
formed in 1948, and the whole inter-American system, which dates back to 1890. For the first time the
concept was accepted that collective intervention in
the affairs of a member was possible under certain
conditions.

This recognition was accorded tacitly in May,
1965, when the Council of the O.A.S. voted in
Washington to create the Inter-American Peace
Force to act in the Dominican Republic. Brazilian,
Paraguayan, Nicaraguan, Honduran and Costa
Rican units were dispatched to assist the United
States troops in peacekeeping activities. A Brazilian
general was named commander of the inter-Amer-

ican force and, as a gesture toward the O.A.S., the
United States commander became his deputy. With
the arrival of the Brazilian contingent, the United
States Marines were withdrawn from the Dominican
Republic a little more than a month after they had
landed there, leaving the 82nd Airborne Division as
the U.S. component of the hemispheric force.

For the O.A.S., traditionally committed to the
hallowed inter-American principle of nonintervention, to agree to collective military action in a Latin-
American country was a most radical departure in
philosophy and practice. This step, taken under the
tremendous pressure of the Dominican civil war,
may strengthen the O.A.S. or weaken it. Only the
future—including the outcome of the Dominican
crisis, still uncertain at this writing—can tell.

On the positive side there is the contention of several governments, including that of the United
States, that the precedent-breaking action in the Dominican situation did no more than force the O.A.S.
finally to face modern realities.

Washington and several other capitals maintain
that the inter-American system must arm itself with
new weapons to counter modern techniques of
Communist subversion. They believe the Inter-
American Peace Force is a guarantee that the hemispheric system can act swiftly against the dangers of
Communist conspiracies.

The opposing view—set forth by a number of

highly articulate and influential governments—is that the abandonment of full respect for the principle of nonintervention may open the door to interventions when the allegation of Communist conspiracy is not necessarily justified. In such cases, this argument runs, inter-American collective actions may favor right-wing or dictatorial governments against democratic or progressive forces.

In the debates on the Dominican crisis in the O.A.S. this view was espoused by Chile, Ecuador, Mexico, Peru and Uruguay—and the resolution creating the inter-American force was approved by the thin majority of one vote. This, of course, underscored the extent of the split in the 20-nation organization.

Chile, Ecuador, Mexico, Peru and Uruguay took the position that Communist involvement in the Dominican rebellion had not been proved and that therefore neither the initial United States intervention nor the subsequent Inter-American Peace Force was justified.

The divergent viewpoints reflect postwar Latin-American political situations.

The United States and some others in the O.A.S. have insisted that the inter-American system has new responsibilities since Cuba came under Communist domination. After several unsuccessful attempts to get the foreign ministers of the O.A.S. members to condemn Cuba for accepting Soviet mil-

itary aid and fostering hemispheric subversion, the
United States obtained a thin-margin vote at the
Punta del Este conference in January, 1962, to ex-
clude the Castro regime from the workings of the
inter-American system. The action was based on the
thesis that Cuba's Marxist-Leninist government was
incompatible with the hemisphere's democratic principles.

At the time of the Cuban missiles crisis in October, 1962, an emergency meeting of the O.A.S.
Council voted unanimously to authorize the United
States blockade of Cuba. This was the only such
unanimous vote—before and since—on Cuba or
the Communist danger in general.

In July, 1964, the O.A.S. took another step
against Cuba. Acting on a Venezuelan complaint
that Cuba had shipped arms for pro-Castro guerrillas seeking to block the November, 1963, Venezuelan elections, the O.A.S. foreign ministers ordered a
series of economic sanctions against Havana.

With this background, then, the 1965 action in
creating the inter-American force for Santo Domingo—and the subsequent plans to set up a permanent force—were a logical consequence of the
earlier moves against Communist subversion.

On the other hand, it must be remembered that
the opponents of the Dominican intervention took
the position that there was no proof of Communist
involvement in Santo Domingo.

The roots of the opposition to the new pattern of collective intervention stemmed from another highly controversial position within the O.A.S. This position is that the inter-American system has the duty of protecting representative democracy from right-wing or military take-overs. After the military coups in Argentina, Peru, Guatemala, Ecuador, the Dominican Republic and Honduras in 1962 and 1963, several governments sought unsuccessfully to have a ministerial conference convened to evolve measures for protecting representative democracy.

In the context of the Dominican crisis, which did so much to alter the whole posture of the O.A.S., the argument advanced by the anti-interventionist forces was that encouragement was being given to dictatorial regimes in the name of anti-Communism.

It appeared significant that four of the five countries opposing the Dominican actions had effective democratic—and anti-Communist—governments. In contrast, more than half of the majority votes came from military or military-backed regimes.

The governments practicing democratic procedures and concentrating on economic and social reforms under the principles of the Alliance for Progress feared that rightist authoritarianism in the name of anti-Communism might subvert their efforts at home.

This was notably true of the new Chilean government of President Eduardo Frei Montalva, who was elected in September, 1964, defeating overwhelmingly a Communist-backed opponent. It was also true of the government of President Fernando Belaúnde Terry in Peru, which in nearly three years of democratic rule and heavy emphasis on development has done much to check Communist-led unrest in the country.

The question being raised by Chile, Peru and several other nations was what precise role the O.A.S. should play in the fast-changing Latin-American scene.

President Frei, in particular, has been insisting that the O.A.S. has become an ossified and unwieldy organization that has failed to throw its full weight into the great battle of Latin-American economic and social development.

Frei and others have felt that greater power should be given to the Inter-American Committee for the Alliance for Progress, which was established in 1964 to coordinate the hemispheric development program. Thus far the committee has little more than an advisory capacity, with the political decisions being made by the Economic and Social Council of the O.A.S., which meets only once a year.

Another point made by the critics of the present activities of the O.A.S. is that insufficient attention is being paid to the possibilities of Latin America's economic integration, or a form of hemispheric common market. Their argument is that neither outside financial investments nor internal efforts can amount to much unless trade problems are solved. The best solution, they say, is a considerable increase in trade within the hemisphere that can be achieved only through the elimination of tariff barriers under a common market.

Carlos Sanz de Santamaría, a jovial but dynamic Colombian who is chairman of the Alliance committee, is advocating additional ideas to aid Latin America's development. An engineer, business leader and former Cabinet minister and Ambassador to the United States, Sanz de Santamaría outlined his views in a recent conversation with me at his Washington office.

"Economic integration and a common market are obviously necessary," he said. "But this will take time—perhaps 10 years—and in the meantime we must push ahead with other steps to make Latin America an economic unit."

Mr. Sanz de Santamaría, who is sometimes called "Mr. Alliance," suggested that duplication of efforts and expenditures by the Latin-American countries was slowing the development process.

For example, he favors a joint campaign to eradicate foot-and-mouth disease in Latin-American cattle herds. He also advocates the establishment of a unified Latin-American airline. In addition, he believes that telecommunications in Latin America

—international telephone service, radio, cable and telex facilities—should be unified to cut costs and increase efficiency.

"Why should a person trying to telephone Guatemala from Colombia have to go through the Miami operator?" he asked.

Mr. Sanz de Santamaría is one of a group of dynamic Latin-American leaders seeking to make what the Alliance for Progress stands for a reality in this generation.

Another is Felipe Herrera, a young Chilean who in five years built the Inter-American Development Bank into one of the world's most successful financial agencies. Actually Mr. Herrera's bank has become much more than a lending institution; it is a center of far-reaching thinking and planning for Latin America's development—with an accent on economic integration—and it has attracted to its staff in Washington some of the most brilliant economic minds in the hemisphere.

José Antonio Mayobre, former Finance Minister of Venezuela, is engaged in a similar effort as executive director of the United Nations Economic Commission for Latin America, which operates out of Santiago, Chile.

At the O.A.S. headquarters in Washington—the ornate Pan American Union building famous for its brilliantly plumed parrots—there are other economic and social planners concentrating on the fu-

ture. They are concerned with the population explosion and birth-control possibilities, with improving
farm techniques and with all the unspectacular but
vital problems of a Latin America bursting at the
seams.

But, as the Dominican crisis emphasized, the
continuing instability of Latin America impedes
these efforts at development. Politics and ideologies
tend to intermix and slow the movement toward
needed reforms. In an extreme case like the Dominican Republic, the 1965 civil war may have set back
for years the patient attempts at rational development. In Bolivia, another strife-torn country, the political upheavals are delaying plans for modernizing
the economy.

What, then, should be the proper role of the Organization of American States?

Despite the controversy over the Dominican situation, most informed people and most governments
agree that the O.A.S. must be strengthened quickly
to deal with the many crises emerging in Latin
America. It is being taken for granted that a new
period of instability lies ahead.

There is a general belief that a mechanism must
be set up to deal with political and security problems
not only on an emergency basis but also through
continuous review.

More power, it is said, should be given to O.A.S.
peacemaking commissions, not only in dire cases

like the Dominican civil war but also in potentially dangerous situations everywhere.

There are experienced diplomats who feel that the O.A.S. should have faced squarely and pushed for a solution of the long-standing border dispute between Peru and Ecuador. This dispute has complicated political and economic cooperation between the two countries and has been continuously exploited by political extremists in both lands.

Likewise, it is said, the O.A.S. should not have left unsettled the 1962 dispute between Bolivia and Chile over the Lauca River. The backlog of unsolved Latin-American problems of this kind includes border situations between Argentina and Chile, the claims of Venezuela against British Guiana, and those of Guatemala against British Honduras.

In the economic and social field a need is felt for a tightening up of organization and procedures under the Alliance for Progress and related programs.

But in the end the O.A.S., like any other international organization, can only be as good as the governments forming it. This means in effect that the time has come for the Latin-American governments to take the O.A.S. more seriously than in the past, when ambassadorships to the organization were often no more than rewards for loyal second-raters or banishments for inconvenient political figures.

VI

The Balance Sheet

WHERE DOES Latin America—and her relationship with the United States—stand in 1965?

There is obviously no single and complete answer to that question, nor is there likely to be one in this generation. The Latin-American revolutionary process, with all its contradictions, emotionalism and ups-and-downs, will color for a long time this vast developing portion of the world. The over-all foreign-policy problems of the United States will also be a factor.

But some rather basic conclusions suggest themselves, even at this juncture of events.

After 10 years of covering Latin America for *The New York Times*—witnessing the bloody revolutions and the hopeful attempts at democratic procedures and economic improvement—these conclusions tend to assert themselves in my mind. And, on the whole, I find myself cautiously optimistic.

Inevitably the dramatic moments of these 10 years form the well-remembered vignettes.

There is the memory of young officers and university students fighting the Perón forces at the outset of the 1955 antidictatorial revolution in Córdoba, Argentina, and the intoxicating explosion of popular joy when the regime was overthrown.

There are the recollections of Colombian and Venezuelan students battling the policemen of the dictatorial regimes and thus setting the stage for the democratic revolutions of the mid-nineteen-fifties.

There is, of course, the unforgettable moment when a Vice President of the United States was nearly lynched in Caracas, Venezuela, in 1958.

And there is the memory of Cuba in the early months of 1959 when Fidel Castro still had his nation believing his victorious revolution would bring political democracy and social justice.

There is the grimness of the Bay of Pigs invasion and of the tense hours when the world stood at the threshold of nuclear war over the Soviet missiles in Cuba.

And, finally, there remain in my memory the terrible days of 1965 in the ancient city of Santo Domingo when Dominicans slaughtered each other in an explosion of fratricidal fury that had its genesis in the Trujillo tyranny.

But there are other memories too—those leading one to the hope that in the end all will be well.

Among them there is first of all that day at the White House—March 13, 1961—when President Kennedy launched the Alliance for Progress, touching off the tremendous initial Latin-American response.

Then there are the memories of the young Latin Americans trying to implement their old hopes for a new future. I am thinking of the Colombian economist who was given an empty desk and the text of the Agrarian Reform Law and was told to "go ahead with the land reform." He did.

I am also thinking of the terribly serious young planners around Peru's President Belaúnde, blueprinting the campaign for wresting arable land from jungle and mountain and teaching Indians how to till the soil.

There is the memory of the new Archbishop of the Brazilian northeast, barely in his forties, telling his bishops and priests that democracy can come only with social justice.

And—very much a part of the new Latin-American scene—there are the Peace Corps volunteers, the young men and women from the United States who have gone to jungle villages and urban slums to befriend the people and teach them with patience and dedication the skills that go into giving man dignity and independence.

And even the statistics are not so discouraging as they may seem at first sight. Actually they tell of a rising per-capita income in a majority of the countries—which is the economists' way of saying that each inhabitant earns each year a little more than he did the year before.

Balancing the violence in Latin America against the hope and the quiet effort that are already changing the face of the region, I am tempted to think that the spectacular drama will before too long be relegated to the history books. But the goals of the work of the planners, the economists, the engineers and the new generation of businessmen may become a living reality for them and their children.

So after a decade of watching Latin America in her revolutionary convulsions and in her indestructible hope that a better future is perhaps just around the corner, I can only share this hope.

INDEX

TAD SZULC

Tad Szulc has reported the news from almost every nation in Latin America as a correspondent for *The New York Times,* and as a member of its Washington bureau he specialized in Latin-American affairs. He is now stationed in Madrid, Spain.

Born in Warsaw in 1926, Mr. Szulc attended school in Switzerland. He joined his father in Rio de Janeiro in 1941, attended the University of Brazil, and then went to work for Associated Press in Brazil. He came to the United States in 1947.

In New York he worked for United Press at the United Nations before joining the staff of *The New York Times* in 1953. After two years as a night rewrite man, Mr. Szulc went to the Far East on a temporary assignment. In the fall of 1955 he was sent to Buenos Aires to cover the Argentine revolt against Perón. Shortly afterward he was named correspondent for *The Times* in Rio de Janeiro.

Based in the Brazilian capital for more than five years, Mr. Szulc was frequently on the move reporting and interpreting events elsewhere on the continent. He has covered revolutions in Venezuela and Cuba, guerrilla warfare in Colombia, conferences in Panama, and dictatorship in Paraguay and the Dominican Republic. In the spring of 1961 Mr. Szulc was transferred to Washington, D.C., where he reported and interpreted government news concerning Latin America.

He is the author of *Twilight of the Tyrants,* a study of the regimes of five South American dictators (1959); with Karl E. Meyer, *The Cuban Invasion* (1962); and *The Winds of Revolution* (1963).